AF255088

The Ultimate Gratitude Journal

*A practical neuroscience approach to rewiring
your brain to be healthier and happier*

Dr Suzanne Henwood and Sarah Carruthers

Published by Luminosity Project Publications; a company created by Dr Suzanne Henwood and Sarah Carruthers that inspires, empowers and supports people to bring the best of who they are to everything they do – to let their light shine, creating a positive ripple effect in the world.

First published in 2022 by Kindle Direct Publishing.

©
All rights reserved.
No part of this publication may be reproduced, stored in any retrieval system, or transmitted by any means, without prior written permission of the authors/copyright holders.

The authors and publishers can accept no legal responsibility for any consequences arising from the application of information, or instructions given in this book.

Copyright belongs to The Luminosity Project Publications
www.theluminosityproject.nz

Wake up, listen to the beating of your heart and create something that will make the world awesome.

Contents

Forward
by Prof Paul Gilbert, OBE

We have come to recognise that humans are a species of great extremes. We can be one of the most violent, vicious, cruel and callous species that have ever walked this planet. A brief glance at history tells of the terrible suffering we have caused other human beings in our wars, tortures, and systematic slavery we have perpetrated and continue to perpetrate.

In February of 2022 the horrors, brutalities and cruelties of war were brought into sharp relief again in Ukraine, although Ukraine is far from the only country that suffers such atrocities. Yet in the same conflicts there are extraordinary examples of people risking their lives to save others and making many sacrifices to help and rescue people. Outside of these contexts, in various rescue services around the world, people know the risks, and some will die saving others.

We tragically lost many of our medical and social care staff trying to save those with COVID-19. On a more local scale, our propensity to help others is probably the most advanced of any species, not just our friends and relations but also at times strangers.

Most acts of helpfulness, where people put themselves out for us are not so serious or costly, thankfully. Nonetheless, being the recipient of another's helpfulness, even minimally, generates positive emotions in us called gratitude. The key to gratitude is for it to be associated with a form of joyfulness or relief rather than obligation. Expressing gratitude shows our appreciation, and receiving the appreciation of others is also a positive experience for the self. It is a reciprocal process where you help me and that stimulates my positive affect and reduces my threat. I show my appreciation which positively impacts you and you show your appreciation of my appreciation. In fact, we now know that this type of social process, like gratitude, is one of the central processes that underpin our extraordinary abilities for caring and sharing. When we compare ourselves to other animals, it is our capacity for sharing and caring in so many ways that set us apart and contributed to our evolutionary success and the evolution of the form of intelligence we now have. Indeed, we have a form of intelligence that makes us particularly interested in being empathic to our own needs and those of others, and in working out how to address them now and in the future. There is no doubt that the evolution of our ability to experience and express gratitude derived from helpfulness, has significantly contributed to human success.

Given that our disposition to be able to experience gratitude has played such a fundamental role in human evolution, it is important to explore how this actually works in the body, its mental and physical health benefits, and how we can train our mind to tap into, and cultivate, those benefits.

In this highly accessible, informative and extremely helpful personal guide, Dr Suzanne Henwood and Sarah Carruthers discuss the profoundly important physiological effects of gratitude and cultivating gratitude. As you will see from their personal disclosures, part of their recognition of the importance of bringing gratitude into one's life comes from a series of major and tragic life events. As they point out, gratitude is not only cultivated by those who have relatively straightforward lives but also for people who struggle in life. Crucially, gratitude is not about dismissing one's pain and suffering, nor entering some of the realms of what one feels one 'ought' or 'should' feel. It is much more about developing the courage and wisdom to be sensitive towards one's reality but also to mindfully focus and train one's attention on what nourishes us rather than depletes us. Moreover, because we now know that the brain can change according to what it practises (called neuroplasticity), when we practise cultivating gratitude, we are also changing our brains and bodies. Gratitude practices have been shown to have profound effects on physiological systems and mental states, and to promote harmonious social relationships.

As with any new skill, there are steps and processes which allow us to begin simply and build up our skills and talents. In this book Dr Suzanne Henwood and Sarah Carruthers guide the reader through some basic gratitude focusing exercises which include gratitude for sensory experience; the ability to take joy from the simple pleasures of life such as the fact that we can see and hear, we can enjoy music and colour, being in nature, watching a sunset, or the pleasure of a cool swim in a calm sea on a hot day. They help us to understand that the ability to take pleasure is partly linked to the ability to feel gratitude for that pleasure, rather than taking it for granted.

As the book unfolds, we are guided through a series of investigations and self-inquiries that invite us to think about our relationship to ourselves and to others in the world we live in. Crucial to the practices is beginning to allow ourselves forms of self-acceptance rather than battling with our minds, criticising ourselves at every turn. Gratitude helps move us from fighting with ourselves to acceptance and developing a genuine compassionate wish to address the sources of our distress, upsets and suffering. Gratitude helps us to recognise the importance of deliberately trying to cultivate opportunities to savour play and bring joy into our lives as best we can.

We have a brain that is tuned to be more sensitive to negativity than to the positive things in life; it is called better safe than sorry. Making deliberate attempts to retune our attention away from its natural tendencies can have very powerful impacts on our mental state.

This book offers a treasure house of insights and opportunities to develop our minds in ways that promote wellbeing and caring social relationships. It is like a fitness gym for the brain with some very good workouts designed to generate life-changing results.

Professor Paul Gilbert, OBE
Developer of Compassion Focused Therapy

Adults who feel grateful have more energy, more optimism, more social connections and more happiness than those who do not. They're also less likely to be depressed, envious, greedy or alcoholics.

MELINDA BECK

Introduction

**W**elcome to The Ultimate Gratitude Journal. The pages to come are specifically designed to help you develop an effective daily gratitude practice based on the neuroscience of gratitude, that will rewire your brain.

Intentionally cultivating gratitude on a daily basis, activates the pro-social circuits in your brain which are designed to bring us closer to ourselves and others, and reduces the defensive circuits associated with backing away, self-isolation or freeze. These pro-social and gratitude circuits are activated when we feel genuine resonance with each other. And the more we are able to put ourselves into another's mindset, the more it changes the wiring of the neural pathways, as well as generating a whole host of other benefits such as increased happiness, a stronger immune system, improved sleep, better emotional regulation, enhanced self-esteem, increased empathy, better relationships, more productivity and increased resilience. But most gratitude practices (e.g. listing things you might be grateful for) are too simplistic and don't actually lead to positive benefits or changes in brain circuitry.

The most *effective* way to galvanise positive change involves stimulating the autonomic nervous system into a state of calm alertness, storytelling and taking in the good. Together these create a neurochemical signature that releases dopamine, oxytocin and serotonin (the feel good chemicals); rewiring your brain; and enabling more effective interactions with yourself and others, so that they become your default way of thinking and being.

The simple structured format of this journal uses all of these elements to help you quickly and easily gain access to these benefits. The more you do it, the more benefits you will gain and the faster you will be able to maintain feeling good as part of who you are.

Our personal journeys with gratitude reached a big crescendo in the last few years.

Suzanne:
In July 2016, on the way home from the airport I got a call from a neighbour to say there were flames coming out of my house and he didn't know where my family were. Physically our family, two cats and two fish, were fine but we lost almost everything we owned. Many people would have been truly challenged to find the good in this and to stop their spiralling negative thoughts from taking control. However, using the process shared in this journal, my family and I got through this ordeal stress free and feeling grateful for what we did have – our faith, the community that supported us, our health, and each other. I wrote a regular 'Phoenix Gratitude Diary' post on facebook to let people know how we were progressing and to keep me focused on the positive. I kept this regular practice going for a year, until we moved back into our home. For me it was a great convincer (on top of the science) of how gratitude can help us bounce back and deal with adversity in a way I would not have believed possible if I hadn't lived through it.

Sarah:
Since February 2019, my husband Rob has suffered from post-concussion syndrome following a mountain bike accident. Then in May 2021, Rob was diagnosed with lung cancer and a few months later, it spread to his brain and back. At the time of writing he has completed 35 days of radiotherapy, three rounds of chemotherapy, two brain surgeries, targeted therapy and an assortment of other treatments for multiple infections. Day by day, we are learning to live with the challenge of Stage IV metastatic cancer (and the side effects of the drugs needed to slow its growth). Throughout these trials, we have had to continually readjust and find a new normal as a family; to do less; take things more slowly; reset the metrics for success; and live "freely and lightly" in a world we are powerless to control. The active daily practice of gratitude as a family alongside our faith has helped bring hope and the ability to cope with our situation. It has made us more positive, joyful, loving, compassionate and energetic. Whilst gratitude hasn't erased the pain, it has helped us build a sort of psychological immune system that has helped us turn hardship (suffering, pain, adversity) into

something fruitful (a life full of new opportunities, gifts and joy) for which we feel profoundly grateful.

A gratitude practice does not make life's challenges go away – it changes your relationship to them. It prevents them from being the main focus in life – enabling you to live life more fully regardless of the circumstances.

If you want more joy, happiness, calm, and connection, and if you want to enjoy and savour every step of the journey then you don't have to wait for a challenge or crisis. As Grant Soosalu used to say, "use where you are now to liberate your human spirit, to reconnect with yourself and bring the best possible version of you into being". Let this be the start of a new wiser way to live your life. And please feel free to let us know how you get on via our website www.theluminosityproject.nz

How to use this Journal

Select a meaningful story. Truly *effective* gratitude practices involve reading or hearing a story (narrative) about someone who received help and associating and experiencing empathy/compassion for that person – for example, stories of people saved during the war, amazing acts of kindness, and going above and beyond what could have been expected. We have included three meaningful stories in this journal on pages 22 and 123. Pick one that really resonates with you or feel free to find/ create your own, as it will become the cornerstone of your daily practice.

Three daily components. 1) Begin each day with gentle, balanced breathing, stimulating your autonomic nervous system into a state of calm alertness. 2) As you continue to breathe deeply and evenly, re-read and reflect on your meaningful story (creating a physiological shift in your heartbeat and breathing). 3) Continuing to savour the feeling of gratitude, write notes on the daily diary pages in your gratitude journal. Each day is numbered and contains six prompts designed to deeply embody your gratitude and establish a positive pattern of thinking, feeling, behaving and being.

These three daily components are designed to permanently tilt your mind towards the good – to activate the pro-social circuits (that draw you closer to others and make you want to lean into life) and reduce the defensive circuits (that keep you safe and make you want to back away from life). Over time, this reduces anxiety and fear pathways, increases motivation and pursuit pathways and draws you closer to others.

Bonus activities. Additional exercises, activities, and challenges are dispersed throughout this Journal as extra gifts to help you stay motivated, build resilience, and remain calm in the face of adversity. You are welcome to dip in and out of these as you like with no pressure to use them on the day suggested. You may also like to use any of the tools (such as breathing) multiple times each day.

Thought-provoking prompts. At the bottom of each page, you will find daily prompts and reflections, designed to inspire you to take in the good through your body's multiple intelligences (heart, head, gut, pelvis, and autonomic nervous system) enabling even deeper embodied wisdom to emerge.

Beauty appreciation. Developing an appreciation of beauty, awe and excellence helps us feel more expansive, positive and grateful. We have therefore included some charming illustrations and colouring pages to encourage you to develop this strength further – to inspire you to fill up on the beautiful things you see, hear, feel, smell and taste in your world. You might also like to notice things in nature/around you as you go about your day.

Habit building. Research tells us that a 100 day challenge should be long enough for you to create the new habit of keeping a gratitude journal and developing an embodied gratitude practice. Knowing there is an end point can help get you started and by the end of 100 days, it's extremely likely that you will have created the neural network infrastructure for it to not only be a daily habit but a must-have! We suggest you set yourself a reminder to follow the process at a specific time of day. We prefer mornings as they set the tone and mindset for the day, but there is no one right time, so do what works for you.

Accountability. You might like to choose a way to make yourself accountable for writing this journal, especially in the first two weeks e.g. a morning reminder in your diary, declare your intention on social media, find an accountability buddy (a person/app) – as we tend to make better choices when we are being watched. Our favourite accountability method is a daily check in with a friend as it both motivates you to build the habit and builds stronger neural networks which super-charge the positive changes in both of your lives. And it's a great way to encourage your friend to get the benefits of gratitude too.

There are only
two ways to
live your life.
One is as though

NOTHING IS A
miracle.

The other
is as though

EVERYTHING IS A
miracle.

ALBERT EINSTEIN

The Power of Gratitude

Have you ever noticed how quickly pleasure fades from your thoughts? How you can do 50 nice things for someone and all they remember is the one thing you didn't do! That no matter how many wonderful things happen to us, we still end up disappointed and find ourselves complaining and fixating on our mistakes!

There's a very good reason for this. Our brain's negativity bias means we tend to remember 'negative experiences' more easily and intensely than positive ones. From an evolutionary point of view, for our species to further itself, we were naturally wired to pay attention to threats to keep ourselves safe. **In effect, the brain is like Velcro for negative experiences, but Teflon for positive ones.**

Consequently, even when positive experiences outnumber negative ones, our stockpile of negative memories naturally grows faster, which can leave us feeling stressed, pessimistic, glum and affect our overall wellbeing. And that's not a fair reflection of reality, as most of our day to day experiences are neutral or positive. Every day, lots of good things happen – you clear your emails, make the subway just before the doors close, someone is kind to you, your favourite song comes on the radio at the perfect moment, you share a smile with a stranger etc.

The good news is that there are many ways we can interrupt our negativity bias and rewire our brains for happiness and positivity. Just like much of our body is built from the foods we eat, our mind is built from the experiences and thoughts we have (and keep having). The flow of experience and thinking gradually sculpts our brain, thus shaping our mind. If we want to reduce our brain's negativity bias we have to learn to take in the good – to foster positive experiences and thinking, until they become a part of who we are.

Gratitude is one of the simplest and most effective ways to retrain our brains.

"Gratitude can make your life happier and more satisfying. When we feel gratitude, we benefit from the pleasant memory of a positive event in our life. Also, when we express our gratitude to others, we strengthen our relationship with them. But sometimes our thank you is said so casually or quickly that it is nearly meaningless... [the key] is to express your gratitude in a thoughtful, purposeful manner" ~ Martin Seligman

Defining Gratitude

Gratitude is a mindset that activates your Prefrontal Cortex (which sets the context and provides meaning to life's experiences), such that it can generate tremendous health and wellbeing benefits. It is a deliberate practice of focusing on, relishing and absorbing the good in our own and others' lives. It is an affirmation of the goodness, gifts and benefits in our lives and the world.

"Gratitude is not just a social construct; it's a real neurobiological phenomenon that is powerful for bringing a deepened sense of well-being, connectedness and enhancing our relationship to self, others and all things" ~ Dr Andrew Huberman

"Gratitude is both an embodied feeling and an action we take. Physically, as we enter a moment of gratitude, our heart rhythms change, our blood pressure drops, our immune function improves, our stress is reduced, and we sleep longer and deeper. Psychologically, we feel more joyful, more alive, more generous, more compassionate, and more connected to others. We experience more life satisfaction and less burnout" - Deb Dana

Research by California University showed that an *effective* gratitude practice has large positive effects on your physical and mental health including an increase in happiness of 25%.

"Gratitude is fertiliser for the mind, spreading connections and improving its function in nearly every realm of experience" ~ Robert Emmons

Robert Emmons' research shows many other positive benefits: physical benefits (stronger immune system, lower blood pressure, less bothered by aches and pains, sleep longer etc.); psychological benefits (improved mood, more joy and pleasure, more alert, alive and awake); social benefits (more helpful, generous and compassionate, more forgiving, more outgoing, lower feelings of loneliness and isolation).

"The neurochemical, anti-inflammatory and the neural circuit mechanisms that gratitude evokes are equally as important as potent forms of intervention like HIIT (High Intensity Interval Training) and can steer your mental and physical health in positive directions, and that those effects are very long-lasting" - Dr Andrew Huberman

Unlike other intentional practices (e.g. mediation, breath work), the positive effects of a gratitude practice can be felt almost instantly (within 60-90 seconds). It immediately reduces defensive circuits and tilts the brain towards more prosocial behaviours.

Antonio Damasio's research shows that our pro-social and gratitude circuits are activated when we feel resonance with another i.e. when we are able to experience the mind of another and know how another person feels (he calls this Theory of Mind). Truly effective gratitude practices are therefore not simply writing down a list of things or thinking about things you are grateful for – it runs deeper than that.

The most potent form of gratitude practice needs to involve story – associating and experiencing empathy/compassion for someone who received help (whether that is help you gave, heard about, or was given to you by someone you connected with). To be effective you must genuinely and emotionally associate with the story, wholeheartedly reflect on it and take it in. In addition, research shows that if you express your gratitude directly to someone who has helped you, it can further increase your sense of happiness by up to 19% (see An Experiment in Gratitude on page 201).

Are you ready to take simple steps to change your brain (positive neuroplasticity) and your life – for the better?

The Ultimate Gratitude Practice

The following amplified, embodied, gratitude process has three daily components:

1. BREATHING:

PET (Positron Emission Tomography) studies show 5-10 minutes of stillness each day, combined with gratitude, creates a neurochemical signature in the body that releases dopamine, serotonin and oxytocin. Dr Andrew Huberman describes this powerful combination as being similar to what *"MDMA or ecstasy is designed to do but without ingesting anything."* A scientifically effective way to quiet ourselves is to use the simple practice of breathing.

There are many styles and practices of breathing. One of the most powerful and relevant here is coherent breathing as it stimulates the autonomic nervous system into a state of calm alertness. So each day your gratitude practice begins with a few minutes of gentle balanced breathing to enhance the positive effects of gratitude. This involves allowing your breath to fall into an easy, deep and even rhythm e.g. six seconds in and six seconds out (or whatever count feels right for you). See the balanced breathing practice on page 20 for more information if this is not familiar for you.

2. GRATITUDE STORY:

As you continue to breathe gently and evenly you bring to mind and feel into your meaningful gratitude story (see the meaningful story section on page 22). Each day you will review your notes on the specifics around it and begin to imagine the story as if you were there now, experiencing it, seeing, feeling, hearing, smelling and tasting it (where relevant). You fill your heart with the story and the positive emotions arising from it (gratitude, loving kindness etc.) then amplify the feelings, sounds and images, making them bigger, stronger, louder, bolder, brighter – just like adjusting the volume/colour on your TV until it's just perfect for you.

3. GRATITUDE JOURNAL:

As you continue to breathe in an even rhythm and focus on the feeling of the strong, positive emotion in your heart, you begin to add notes to your journal using the diary created to support you. This may include additional stories about others or the help you are grateful for in your life, other positive things in your life, positive changes, growth areas etc. We suggest you follow the simple yet deeply embodied mBraining process with an example of how to fill it in on page 29 to support you in this. Please see the resource list on page 202 for more information on mBraining.

Recommended Minimum Daily Dose: 5 mins per day.

Gratitude is a self-transcendent emotion
– it lifts us out of the everyday and expands our perspective,
which helps us get along with each other better.

1) Balanced Breathing Practice

---

ndrew Weil says that *"improper breathing is a common cause of ill health. If I had to limit my advice on healthier living to just one tip, it would be simply to learn how to breathe correctly. There is no single more powerful – or more simple – daily practice to further your health and well being than breathwork"*.

To practise balanced breathing, start by finding a comfortable seated position with a straight spine. Relax your tongue and your jaw. Then tenderly bring your awareness to your breath. If you aren't already, breathe deeply, yet softly, in and out through your nose.

If you can, allow your in-breath to slowly and gently fill your belly. On your out-breath allow your belly to deflate. As you continue to breathe from your belly, focus on your natural breathing pattern and begin to count the length (number of seconds) of each inhale and exhale to obtain a baseline.

As you continue to breathe in the same way, begin to gently slow down your breathing so it forms a deep and even rhythm (without pauses) e.g. six seconds in and six seconds out (or whatever count feels just right where the in and out-breath are the same number of seconds in and out).

As you breathe, place your hand over your heart and shift your focus to that area. Imagine your breath is flowing in and out of your heart or chest area. Now bring your awareness to something or someone you deeply appreciate. Really feel that appreciation and notice the sensations, images, colours, sounds and feelings. If you begin by 'thinking' about the feeling, bring your focus back to the heart area to really 'feel' the feeling. Just enjoy being in this space and resting in this awareness. Notice there is no effort here, just open spacious awareness.

If you breathe in this balanced, coherent way for 2-5 minutes the rhythm will change your Heart Rate Variability, taking you into a beautiful place of calm alertness (flow) and inner connection. It is also a great place to learn and make decisions from. If you would like to listen to a recording of the balanced breathing process check out bit.ly/3PRn7L9

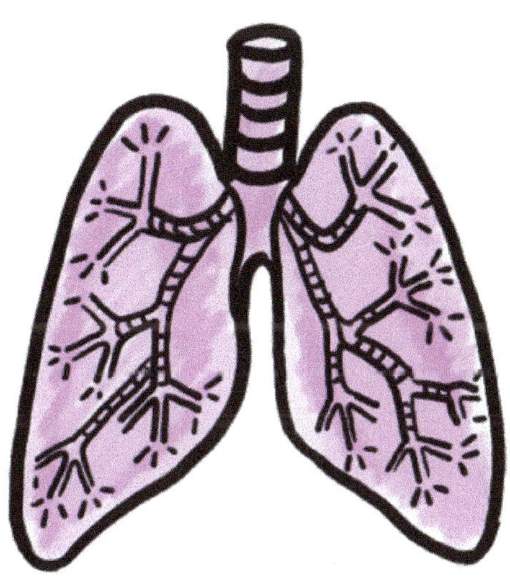

2) Select a Meaningful Story

The second part of your daily practice involves bringing to mind and feeling into your meaningful gratitude story – a powerful story that (after distilling into a few bullet points) you then repeat after your breathing in each practice (taking a shortcut to activate your pro-social gratitude circuits).

The story you choose needs to be one that resonates with you and involves someone either giving or receiving help. It could be yourself or someone that inspires you from a book/podcast/movie. Ideally the person in the story overcomes a struggle and feels genuine gratitude for the help. Examples of stories you might like to use are on page 25, 26 and 123 or you can find a recording at bit.ly/3PRn7L9

From your chosen story, jot down a few bullet points about how you perceive the person who experienced the struggle felt as they overcame their challenges. What help did they get/give? How does this make YOU feel? (e.g. resonance, empathy, compassion etc.) Imagining this Theory of Mind enables the gratitude circuits in your Prefrontal Cortex to light up.

Gently bring awareness to your breath, breathing deeply and evenly in and out of the belly. Slowly shift your in and out-breath into a deep and even rhythm e.g. six seconds in and six seconds out (or an even count that is just right for you) as per the balanced breathing instructions on page 20.

Continue to gently breathe in this rhythm, bring to mind and feel into the meaningful story you chose. Re-read your bullet points and recall the specifics of the story – if you can, visualise a movie/image of the person/scene, identify key words or sounds associated with it, feel into the sensations. Take your time to really tune into the most resonant parts of the story and experiences around it.

Now bring your attention into the area surrounding your heart. Place the palm of your right hand over your heart. Begin to amplify the feelings of gratitude associated with this experience and with overcoming the struggle. If there are colours/images/shapes make them brighter/more vivid; if there are sounds make them louder; if there is movement increase it; if there is texture magnify it until it feels just perfectly right for you. Let the unique characteristics of this beautiful sensation of gratitude flow from your heart, really embracing the experience – like water soaking into a sponge. Do this for at least thirty seconds (research shows this is the minimum time required for it to have a lasting impact on us).

Now drop your attention into your abdomen and pause to answer the question *"Who is the you, that is deeply grateful?"* Take a moment to bring the gratitude you are feeling into that part and to deeply savour it. What lessons have you learned from (re-) imagining overcoming this struggle/empathising with others? How has it impacted you? For example, does it inspire you to work harder, keep going, try something new? What else have you learnt about who you are as you reimagine the beauty of the human spirit in this story?

Allow the feeling of gratitude to grow and spread around your whole body – feeling the sensations expand in a way that is beautifully right for you, all the way to your skin's surface. You might even like to gently stroke your skin in a way that feels delicious (e.g. your arms/palm of your hands/face) to connect with them even more deeply, as you appreciate and acknowledge them throughout your entire body.

Lastly move your attention back to your heart, bringing with it all the awareness that you have perceived. As you do this, truly appreciate whatever it was you were grateful for, in an even deeper way. Ask yourself *"What is new and different now?"*

"Stories create community, enable us to see through the eyes of other people, and open us to the claims of others."
- Peter Forbes

Meaningful Story Examples

A powerful gratitude story needs to be one that really inspires and resonates with you, is based on someone overcoming a struggle and involves associating with and experiencing empathy/compassion for the person who received help (whether it's the help you gave or help you read/heard about). Below are some examples you might like to use, or some prompts to help you to create your own.

Story 1: Random acts of kindness
One Friday afternoon, Rachel, a working mum of two, got a call to say her husband Doug had been taken to hospital following a heart attack. She desperately wanted to be by his side, but her kids needed to be picked up from school and as they had just moved area, she didn't know who to ask.

She decided to take a risk and rang a lady she had recently met at the school gate – Diane who had welcomed her a few weeks before. Diane dropped everything and immediately went to pick up the kids. Diane reassured the kids, drove them back to her house, gave them dinner and a bath and made up the spare beds so they could stay over.

When Rachel arrived at the hospital, she discovered Doug required surgery and would be in hospital for at least a week. People she hardly knew rallied around her – organising school drop offs/pick ups, school lunches, dinners, lifts to hospital, picking up Doug's car from work, cutting her lawn, laundry etc. This enabled Rachel to spend time with Doug in hospital, and once he was home, it supported them as a family. Throughout the three months it took Doug to fully recover, Rachel felt comforted, held and loved. She was amazed at how people had helped, easing her stress and protecting her children. She didn't know how she could have got through those weeks on her own and knew that she would never be able to return the favour to so many kind people.

Jot down: What are the main points of note in this story? What was the struggle? How did others help? What is the emotional impact of this story on you? Imagine you were Rachel, how would you feel? Imagine you were one of the people who helped without expecting anything in return? What do you experience?

Story 2: Seven mile ride*

After leaving a store, Clarence, an older gentleman, returned to his car only to find that he had locked his keys and cell phone inside. A teenager (who was not known to Clarence) was riding past on his bike and saw Clarence kick a tyre and say a few choice words (clearly showing some distress). *"What's wrong?"* he asked. Clarence explained his situation and that he couldn't call his wife and ask her to bring the spare car key as they only had one car, and she could not get it to him. The teenager passed him his phone and said, *"Call your wife and tell her I'm coming to get her key."* Clarence said, *"But that's seven miles round trip".* *"Don't worry about it"* the teenager insisted and Clarence called his wife. An hour later, the teenager returned with the key. Clarence offered him some money, wanting to express his sincere gratitude, but the teenager refused. *"Let's just say I needed the exercise,"* he said. Then, like a cowboy in the movies, he rode off into the sunset.

Jot down: What are the main points of note in this true story? What was the struggle? How did the teenager help? How did it make you feel? Imagine you were Clarence or the teenager, how would you feel? What is the emotional impact of this story on you?

Story 3: Create your own

Remember a time when you helped alleviate someone's pain, or simply made someone's life better. Think about and feel into how it impacted you supporting them? If they thanked you, what was it like to receive genuine thanks? What did you see, hear and feel? Really tune into the feelings/sensations you got from genuinely helping someone.

Jot down notes on this.

Or perhaps you can remember a time when you were blown away by someone that helped you. What did they do? What did you see, hear and feel? Think about how it impacted you personally and how you felt before and after the help? What was the emotional impact of this story on you?

Jot down notes on this. And remember, expressing your gratitude to them will help them feel great AND increase your happiness.

Note: There are some empty pages at the back of this journal for you to jot down your story notes.

**Clarence W. Stephens, Kentucky*

3) The Gratitude Journal

After you have filled your heart with your meaningful story, you can deeply embody and broaden your gratitude so it includes the little and the big things in your daily life. You can then add notes in your journal using the daily diary.

Shift your attention from your **HEART** to your **HEAD** as you continue to breathe gently and evenly. Bring to mind the specifics of what you are grateful for today – an image/movie, key word(s)/phrase(s)/sound(s) associated with it e.g. your morning coffee, the sound of the rain etc. Really dive into the detail, the stories and meaning surrounding it.

Now bring your attention back into the area surrounding your **HEART.** Really tune into your feelings of gratitude. If there are colours or images make them brighter / more vivid; if there are sounds make them louder; if there is movement increase it; if there is texture magnify it; amplify the feelings until they are just right. Really feel into all the unique characteristics of this beautiful sensation of gratitude. Let your heart absorb the experience like water soaking into a sponge for at least thirty seconds.

Drop your attention into your **GUT** and pause to answer the question *"Who is the you, that is deeply grateful?"* Take a moment to bring the gratitude into that part and to deeply savour it.

Allow the feeling of gratitude to grow and spread around your whole **BODY** – feeling the sensations in a way that feels beautifully right for you. Let the sensations go out to your **SKIN** surface (and maybe even beyond). You might even like to gently stroke your skin (e.g. arms/palm of your hands/face) in a way that feels delicious and enables you to connect with that feeling even more deeply, as you appreciate and acknowledge this awareness through your entire body.

Lastly bring your attention back to your heart, bringing with it all the awareness and learnings – **INTEGRATING** them into all of who you are. As you do this, truly appreciate whatever it was that you were grateful for in an even deeper way. Ask yourself *"What is new and different now?"* Then write your Gratitude reflections in your daily Journal page. On the right is a sample page to give you an idea of what a completed day might look like.

You now have everything you need to begin – coherent breathing, a meaningful story and your journal. Congratulations on taking the first step to becoming more grateful and intentionally cultivating wellbeing, connectedness and better relationships. Feel free to let your imagination run loose, your curiosity and sense of discovery rule as you make the journal your own using words, colour, doodles and images to take your gratitude in any direction you choose. Allow yourself time to drop deep into your chosen story, to follow the prompt questions and process each day and really *feel* the gratitude flow through your entire body.

*"When I think about gratitude practices, I think about
the ripple effect that comes from throwing a stone
in the water. One moment of gratitude, one simple
act of goodness, ripples out to reach others one by one"*
- Deb Dana

Date: Saturday 2nd Feb   **Today's Context:** Long weekend

Pause. Take a moment to feel into your meaningful story.
Breathe evenly and focus on your heart:

Things I feel truly grateful for:

The smell of a new book, my morning coffee, falling asleep to the sound of the rain, alone time, my fav song.

Because...

It is the ordinary things that make life extraordinary.

What positive story will I tell:

The story I am telling myself now is that I am already focusing on ways that life is good right now.

I am starting the day grounded in gratitude and choosing to appreciate the small as well as the big things

I can express my gratitude by:

Shout out to a friend.

Naming what I am grateful for.

Showing enthusiasm and varying my vocabulary when I say thank you e.g. "I appreciate you", "this means a lot to me", "you are so thoughtful".

I can choose to focus on:

Seeking out all the good things in my life and practicing expressing appreciation.

Focus on my strengths and how I can maintain healthy habits today - 30 min walk, 8 hours sleep, one minute breathing meditation each hour.

The difference I will make:

Aim for one Random Act of Kindness today.

Ask people how they are and actively listen to their response.

Label my emotions to lessen their impact

3 key emotions for me today:

Joy (sense of elation, happiness, gladness as I notice something).

Hope (optimism and anticipation about a positive future).

Serenity (calm and peaceful feeling of acceptance of me and what I have).

Take a moment to be grateful for the kindness of strangers
– those that hold open doors, smile across the street
or let you into their lane when you drive.

Understanding where you are now

As you begin this journey, we suggest you take a moment to reflect on how life is for you right now. There is no right or wrong answer, just your reality. See this as a starting point to come back to and reflect on, so you can track your growth over time.

On the chart below, mark for each statement, where you are on the scale: from 1 (strongly disagree), 2 (disagree), 3 (slightly disagree), 4 (neutral), 5 (slightly agree), 6 (agree) to 7 (strongly agree).*

	1	2	3	4	5	6	7
1. I have so much in life to be thankful for							
2. If I had to list everything that I felt grateful for, it would be a very long list							
3. When I look at the world, I don't see much to be grateful for							
4. I am grateful to a wide variety of people							
5. As I get older I find myself more able to appreciate the people, events, and situations that have been part of my life history							
6. Long amounts of time can go by before I feel grateful to something or someone							

Calculate your total score, by adding up each individual score of each question. Note that the scores from questions 3 and 6 are reverse-scored (i.e. count as a negative statement), so if the score in the first column is 7 then the score in the last column might be 1. Divide your total score by 6 to give you an average score. If you need more advice on scoring please visit bit.ly/3PRn7L9

Record your score here:

*Source: The Gratitude Questionnaire-Six-Item Form (GQ-6) by McCullough, M. E., Emmons, R. A., & Tsang, J.

GRATITUDE turns what we have into enough, and more. It turns DENIAL into ACCEPTANCE, CHAOS into ORDER, CONFUSION into CLARITY. It makes sense of today, and creates a vision for TOMORROW.

MELODY BEATTIE

Desired Outcome

Having a clear goal / outcome is important to know where you are heading. The best way to identify this is to firstly bring your body into calm alertness via balanced breathing (breathing evenly and deeply using your belly, ideally six seconds in and six seconds out).

"If you have a goal, write it down,
If you do not write it down,
you do not have a goal
you have a wish"
- Steve Maraboli

Think about, feel into and identify what specifically you want to achieve over the next 100 days? If you can, write down **three key outcomes** on the opposite page. State each one in the positive i.e. what you want (not what you don't want). Consider things like when, where and with whom you want it to occur.

Then for each one, identify what is important to you about each outcome and what achieving that outcome will allow you to be/do.

"By recording your dreams and goals on paper,
you set in motion the process of becoming
the person you most want to be.
Put your future in good hands – your own"
- Mark Victor Hansen

Outcome 1:

This is important because:

This will allow me to:

Outcome 2:

This is important because:

This will allow me to:

Outcome 3:

This is important because:

This will allow me to:

Date: **Today's Context:**
Pause. Take a moment to feel into your meaningful story.
Breathe evenly and focus on your heart:

Things I feel truly grateful for:

Because...

What positive story will I tell:

I can express my gratitude by:

I can choose to focus on:

The difference I will make:

3 key emotions for me today:

The more grateful you become, the easier it is to be grateful.

Date: **Today's Context:**

Pause. Take a moment to feel into your meaningful story.
Breathe evenly and focus on your heart:

Things I feel truly grateful for:

Because...

What positive story will I tell:

I can express my gratitude by:

I can choose to focus on:

The difference I will make:

3 key emotions for me today:

*Imagine what life would be like without certain people or things,
and consider how they helped you.*

Date: **Today's Context:**

Pause. Take a moment to feel into your meaningful story.
Breathe evenly and focus on your heart:

Things I feel truly grateful for:

Because...

What positive story will I tell:

I can express my gratitude by:

I can choose to focus on:

The difference I will make:

3 key emotions for me today:

*"The more you express gratitude for what you have, the more
likely you will have even more to express gratitude for"*
~ Zig Ziglar

Date: **Today's Context:**

Pause. Take a moment to feel into your meaningful story.
Breathe evenly and focus on your heart:

Things I feel truly grateful for:

Because...

What positive story will I tell:

I can express my gratitude by:

I can choose to focus on:

The difference I will make:

3 key emotions for me today:

*"If the only prayer you said in your whole
life was, Thank You, that would suffice"
~ Meister Eckhart*

Date: **Today's Context:**

Pause. Take a moment to feel into your meaningful story.
Breathe evenly and focus on your heart:

Things I feel truly grateful for:

Because...

What positive story will I tell:

I can express my gratitude by:

I can choose to focus on:

The difference I will make:

3 key emotions for me today:

Take the time to really look to each side – left and right.
Observe details you normally overlook and gaze at
them with a sense of wonder.

Date: **Today's Context:**

Pause. Take a moment to feel into your meaningful story.
Breathe evenly and focus on your heart:

Things I feel truly grateful for:

Because...

What positive story will I tell:

I can express my gratitude by:

I can choose to focus on:

The difference I will make:

3 key emotions for me today:

"Thank you" is the best prayer that anyone could say.
I say that one a lot. Thank you expresses extreme
gratitude, humility, understanding"
~ Alice Walker

Date: **Today's Context:**

Pause. Take a moment to feel into your meaningful story.
Breathe evenly and focus on your heart:

Day 7

Things I feel truly grateful for:

Because...

What positive story will I tell:

I can express my gratitude by:

I can choose to focus on:

The difference I will make:

3 key emotions for me today:

*"Thankfulness is the beginning of gratitude. Gratitude
is the completion of thankfulness. Thankfulness may
consist merely of words. Gratitude is shown in acts"
~ Henri Frederic Amiel*

Bonus Activity

When was the last time you explored your values? Values indicate what is important to you (or not important). They are the core criteria you hold about why something is worthwhile, what you perceive is right and wrong, what you feel is good and bad, what is true for you. Your values motivate you. They determine how you spend your time. They sit at heart level and drive your behaviours and attention.

Take a moment to bring your breathing into balance. Put your hand on your heart and connect with a positive emotion such as compassion or loving kindness. As you breathe, ask your heart what is your CORE VALUE? What is it you value most? e.g. integrity, respect, authenticity etc. Write whatever comes up for you in the centre of the heart below.

Take a moment to reflect on what this means in your life right now. How does this value direct your attention? How does it change what you do? How does it change how you feel? Write all the words you can think of related to this value around the heart below.

Count your gifts.
Relish and savour the things you have received.

Seven Days in Review

Well done for completing your first seven days. Take a moment to reflect on your achievements and to acknowledge your investment in YOU. Look back over your Journal entries from this week.

What are your key learnings, insights and discoveries from this week?

What changes in yourself have you been aware of? E.g. behaviours, focus, emotional state/mood etc.

What will you do differently next week?

"When gratitude becomes your default setting, life changes"
~ Nancy Leigh Demoss

Sometimes
we put up walls.
Not to keep
people out,
but to see who
cares enough
to knock
them down.

Date: **Today's Context:**

Pause. Take a moment to feel into your meaningful story. Breathe evenly and focus on your heart:

Things I feel truly grateful for:

Because...

What positive story will I tell:

I can express my gratitude by:

I can choose to focus on:

The difference I will make:

3 key emotions for me today:

"Enjoy the little things, for one day you may look back and realise they were the big things"
~ Robert Braul

Date: **Today's Context:**

Pause. Take a moment to feel into your meaningful
story. Breathe evenly and focus on your heart:

Things I feel truly grateful for:

Because...

What positive story will I tell:

I can express my gratitude by:

I can choose to focus on:

The difference I will make:

3 key emotions for me today:

*Ever notice that the first bite of chocolate is
always the best? Try abstaining from something
for a week and then see how it feels!*

Date: **Today's Context:**
Pause. Take a moment to feel into your meaningful
story. Breathe evenly and focus on your heart:

Things I feel truly grateful for:

Because...

What positive story will I tell:

I can express my gratitude by:

I can choose to focus on:

The difference I will make:

3 key emotions for me today:

"Feeling gratitude and not expressing it is like
wrapping a present and not giving it"
~ William Arthur Ward

Pause. Take a moment to feel into your meaningful
story. Breathe evenly and focus on your heart:

Things I feel truly grateful for:

Because...

What positive story will I tell:

I can express my gratitude by:

I can choose to focus on:

The difference I will make:

3 key emotions for me today:

Look out of your window.
What are you truly grateful for?

Date: **Today's Context:**

Pause. Take a moment to feel into your meaningful
story. Breathe evenly and focus on your heart:

Things I feel truly grateful for:

Because...

What positive story will I tell:

I can express my gratitude by:

I can choose to focus on:

The difference I will make:

3 key emotions for me today:

Look in a mirror and see what others see.
What are you deeply grateful for about you?

49

Date: **Today's Context:**

Pause. Take a moment to feel into your meaningful story. Breathe evenly and focus on your heart:

Things I feel truly grateful for:

Because...

What positive story will I tell:

I can express my gratitude by:

I can choose to focus on:

The difference I will make:

3 key emotions for me today:

"The roots of all goodness lie in the soil of appreciation for goodness"
~ Dalai Lama

Date: **Today's Context:**

Pause. Take a moment to feel into your meaningful
story. Breathe evenly and focus on your heart:

Things I feel truly grateful for:

Because...

What positive story will I tell:

I can express my gratitude by:

I can choose to focus on:

The difference I will make:

3 key emotions for me today:

Take the time to really look up, down and behind you.
Observe details you normally overlook and
gaze at them with a sense of child-like curiosity.

Bonus Activity

Go online and search for the positive benefits of Gratitude. Create a list of what you find (feel free to make notes around what emerges for you as you read and focus on each benefit). Which of these benefits are you already experiencing? And which would you like more of? Highlight/ underline those.

"The way to develop the best that is in a person is by appreciation and encouragement"
- Charles Schwab

14 Days in Review

Well done for completing 14 days. Take a moment to reflect on your achievements and to acknowledge your investment in YOU. Look back over your Journal entries from this week.

What are your key learnings, insights and discoveries from this week?

What changes in yourself have you been aware of? E.g. behaviours, focus, emotional state/mood etc.

What will you do differently next week?

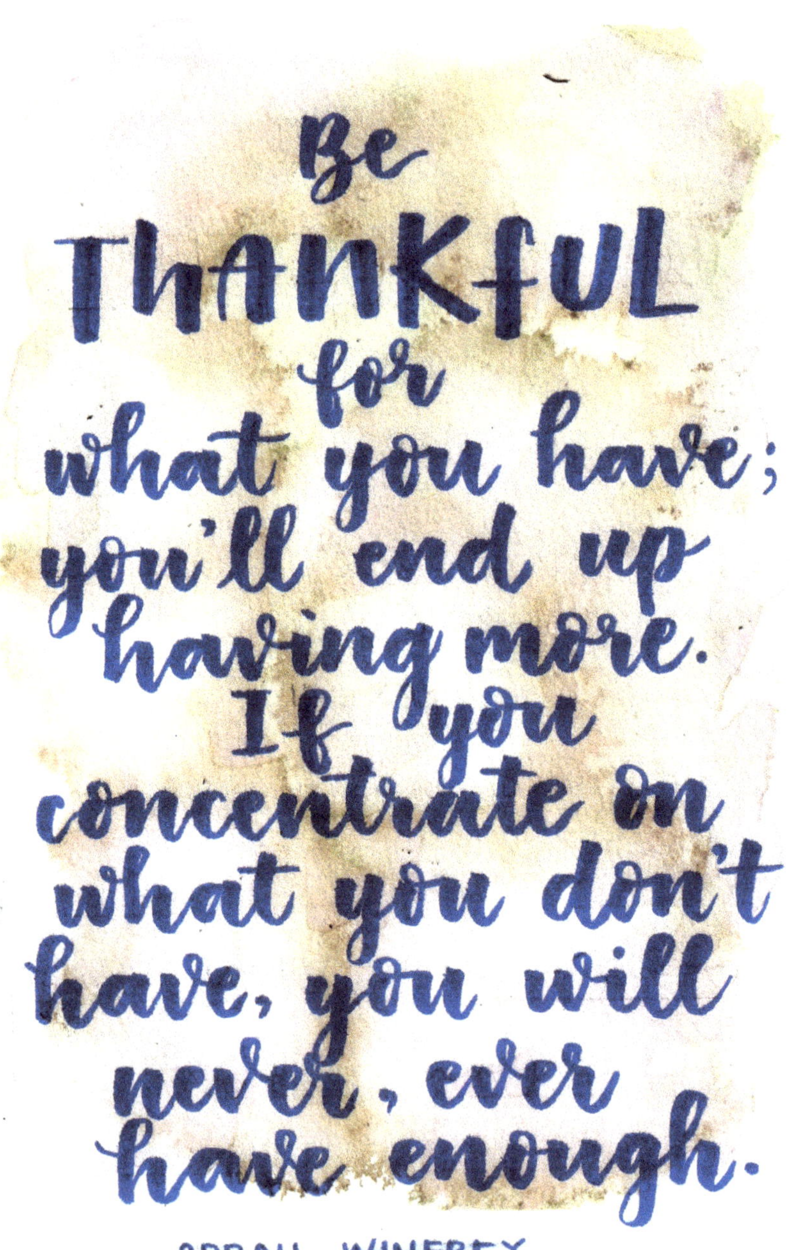

Be
THANKFUL
for
what you have;
you'll end up
having more.
If you
concentrate on
what you don't
have, you will
never, ever
have enough.

OPRAH WINFREY

Date: **Today's Context:**

Pause.   Take a moment to feel into your meaningful story.
Breathe evenly and focus on your heart:

Things I feel truly grateful for:

Because...

What positive story will I tell:

I can express my gratitude by:

I can choose to focus on:

The difference I will make:

3 key emotions for me today:

Look up at the sky. What do you notice?
What surprises and delights you?

Date: **Today's Context:**

Pause. Take a moment to feel into your meaningful story.
Breathe evenly and focus on your heart:

Things I feel truly grateful for:

Because...

What positive story will I tell:

I can express my gratitude by:

I can choose to focus on:

The difference I will make:

3 key emotions for me today:

*"Reflect upon your present blessings, of which every
man has plenty; not on your past misfortunes,
of which all men have some"*
- Charles Dickens

Date: **Today's Context:**

Pause. Take a moment to feel into your meaningful story.
Breathe evenly and focus on your heart:

Things I feel truly grateful for:

Because...

What positive story will I tell:

I can express my gratitude by:

I can choose to focus on:

The difference I will make:

3 key emotions for me today:

Take the time to really gaze at your marvellous hands.
What makes them special? What are you appreciative of?

Date: **Today's Context:**

Pause. Take a moment to feel into your meaningful story.
Breathe evenly and focus on your heart:

Things I feel truly grateful for:

Because...

What positive story will I tell:

I can express my gratitude by:

I can choose to focus on:

The difference I will make:

3 key emotions for me today:

"None is more impoverished than the one who has no gratitude. Gratitude is a currency that we can mint for ourselves and spend without fear of bankruptcy"
- Fred De Witt Van Amburgh

Date: **Today's Context:**

Pause. Take a moment to feel into your meaningful story.
Breathe evenly and focus on your heart:

Things I feel truly grateful for:

Because...

What positive story will I tell:

I can express my gratitude by:

I can choose to focus on:

The difference I will make:

3 key emotions for me today:

Listen to the sounds around you right now.
What can you hear as you truly listen to the
present moment and what it beholds?

Pause. Take a moment to feel into your meaningful story.
Breathe evenly and focus on your heart:

Things I feel truly grateful for:

Because...

What positive story will I tell:

I can express my gratitude by:

I can choose to focus on:

The difference I will make:

3 key emotions for me today:

"Some people grumble that roses have thorns;
I am grateful that thorns have roses"
- Alphonse Karr

Date: **Today's Context:**

Pause. Take a moment to feel into your meaningful story.
Breathe evenly and focus on your heart:

Things I feel truly grateful for:

Because...

What positive story will I tell:

I can express my gratitude by:

I can choose to focus on:

The difference I will make:

3 key emotions for me today:

Really sense your heart awakening to gratitude today.
Let it fill every part of your heart until it glows.

21 Days in Review

Well done for completing 21 days. Take a moment to reflect on your achievements and to acknowledge your investment in YOU. Look back over your Journal entries from this week.

What are your key learnings, insights and discoveries from this week?

What changes in yourself have you been aware of? E.g. behaviours, focus, emotional state/mood etc.

What will you do differently next week?

Turn a tap in your house and listen to the beautiful sound made by the water. What are you grateful for?

Bonus Activity

Pause. Before reading on, feel into your body and notice what you are feeling right now? Perhaps you are curious/hopeful/annoyed/distracted/sad? Emotions are part of human nature. They give us information about what we are experiencing and they drive our behaviour. Therefore the more you can notice and name your emotions, the more regulated you are when reacting to them. This makes it easier to: understand your emotional responses; deal with life's challenges; resolve conflicts; and move past challenging feelings.

There are at least 34,000 different distinguishable feelings (Goleman and Dali Lama, 2004). Yet most of us operate with only 12-16 on a daily basis. Just like anything else in life, you can improve your emotional awareness through practice. One way to do this is when you become aware of an emotion, to pause and feel into it. Name it and describe its' characteristics, strength and where in your body you can feel it. Over time, by getting more specific about what you are aware of, you can distinguish between different and similar emotions and label them more accurately. Let's have a practice now ...

Take a moment to highlight/circle, how you _don't_ want to feel:

Afraid	Alienated	Alone	Annoyed
Anxious	Blocked	Closed	Confused
Confused	Defensive	Diminished	Disconnected
Disheartened	Doubtful	Embarrassed	Guarded
Hesitant	Incapable	Inferior	Insulted
Insecure	Intimidated	Intolerant	Impatient
Judged	Neglect	Overwhelmed	Paralysed
Powerless	Reactive	Rebellious	Restless
Stuck	Uncaring	Uncomfortable	Unwelcome

With self compassion, for each of those you have highlighted/circled, be really honest and write down a list of actions of what you would need to DO to ensure you do not feel those undesired emotions.

Now take a moment to highlight/circle how you _do_ want to feel:

Appreciated	Attentive	Brave	Caring
Carefree	Confident	Connected	Compassionate
Courageous	Curious	Daring	Delighted
Easygoing	Empathetic	Encouraged	Energised
Equal	Fascinated	Free	Fun loving
Grateful	Helpful	Humble	Inspired
Involved	Joy	Kind	Lighthearted
Loving	Non-judgemental	Open	Open-minded
Optimistic	Playful	Proud	Purposeful
Rebellious	Restless	Secure	Serene
Spontaneous	Supported	Thoughtful	Uncomfortable
Understanding	Unique	Welcome	Wonder

Think and feel into what you specifically need to do in order to feel more of those emotions. Write this down.

For more games and resources on emotions, check out The Emotional Culture Deck at https://www.ridersandelephants.com

"While gratitude is both a feeling and an attitude, thankfulness is the demonstrative expression of it, whether extended to ourselves or others"
- Angeles Arrien

Gratitude is the healthiest of all human emotions. The more you express gratitude for what you have, the more likely you will have even more (to) express gratitude (for).

-ZIG ZIGLAR

Date: **Today's Context:**

Pause. Take a moment to feel into your meaningful story.
Breathe evenly and focus on your heart:

Things I feel truly grateful for:

Because...

What positive story will I tell:

I can express my gratitude by:

I can choose to focus on:

The difference I will make:

3 key emotions for me today:

*"I would maintain that thanks are the highest form of thought;
and that gratitude is happiness doubled by wonder"*
~ G.K. Chesterton

Date: **Today's Context:**
Pause. Take a moment to feel into your meaningful story.
Breathe evenly and focus on your heart:

Things I feel truly grateful for:

Because...

What positive story will I tell:

I can express my gratitude by:

I can choose to focus on:

The difference I will make:

3 key emotions for me today:

Consider the people who have helped you get where you are today.
Who would you like to thank and what for?
Consider writing a letter/note to tell them.

Date: **Today's Context:**
Pause. Take a moment to feel into your meaningful story.
Breathe evenly and focus on your heart:

Things I feel truly grateful for:

Because...

What positive story will I tell:

I can express my gratitude by:

I can choose to focus on:

The difference I will make:

3 key emotions for me today:

"Enjoy the little things, for one day you may look
back and realise they were the big things"
~ Robert Brault

Date: **Today's Context:**

Pause. Take a moment to feel into your meaningful story.
Breathe evenly and focus on your heart:

Things I feel truly grateful for:

Because...

What positive story will I tell:

I can express my gratitude by:

I can choose to focus on:

The difference I will make:

3 key emotions for me today:

*If you could shift your awareness to being grateful for the
sense of sight, how would you see things differently today?*

Date: **Today's Context:**
Pause. Take a moment to feel into your meaningful story.
Breathe evenly and focus on your heart:

Things I feel truly grateful for:

Because...

What positive story will I tell:

I can express my gratitude by:

I can choose to focus on:

The difference I will make:

3 key emotions for me today:

If you find yourself repeating the same things, focus on what
specifically is 'new and different' about them today. What descriptive
words, images, sounds, smells and tastes can you add?

Date: **Today's Context:**

Pause. Take a moment to feel into your meaningful story.
Breathe evenly and focus on your heart:

Things I feel truly grateful for:

Because...

What positive story will I tell:

I can express my gratitude by:

I can choose to focus on:

The difference I will make:

3 key emotions for me today:

*"He is a wise man who does not grieve for the things
which he has not, but rejoices for those which he has"*
- Epictetus

Date: **Today's Context:**

Pause. Take a moment to feel into your meaningful story.
Breathe evenly and focus on your heart:

Things I feel truly grateful for:

Because...

What positive story will I tell:

I can express my gratitude by:

I can choose to focus on:

The difference I will make:

3 key emotions for me today:

*Go outside and listen to the amazing cacophony
of sounds. What are you grateful for?*

Gratitude

is not a passive response to something we have been given. GRATITUDE arises from paying attention, from being awake in the presence of everything that lives within and without us.

DAVID WHITE

Bonus Activity

If you were an animal/plant what would you be? Use the space below to draw it.

What qualities does that animal/plant have? What does that animal/ plant represent? What lessons could it be trying to teach you about your own personal power and inner strength? E.g. a cat might represent curiosity, adventure, independence, patience...

Strengths are things that help people cope with adversity and find fulfilment in life. They can include qualities, talents, gifts, knowledge, skills etc. Write down your strengths/what you do well. For each one, note how it is useful to you and how you might develop them/use a little more often/transfer into other areas of you life.

28 Days in Review

Well done for completing 28 days. Take a moment to reflect on your achievements and to acknowledge your investment in YOU. Look back over your Journal entries from this week.

What are your key learnings, insights and discoveries from this week?

What changes in yourself have you been aware of? E.g. behaviours, focus, emotional state/mood etc.

What will you do differently next week?

Date: **Today's Context:**

Pause. Take a moment to feel into your meaningful story.
Breathe evenly and focus on your heart:

Things I feel truly grateful for:

Because...

What positive story will I tell:

I can express my gratitude by:

I can choose to focus on:

The difference I will make:

3 key emotions for me today:

Learning to meet the resistance that gratitude awakens is part of the process. Be gentle as you open yourself up and surrender to it.

78

Date: **Today's Context:**

Pause. Take a moment to feel into your meaningful story.
Breathe evenly and focus on your heart:

Things I feel truly grateful for:

Because...

What positive story will I tell:

I can express my gratitude by:

I can choose to focus on:

The difference I will make:

3 key emotions for me today:

*"Gratefulness is the inner gesture of giving
meaning to our life by receiving life as a gift"
~ Brother David Steindl-Rast*

Pause. Take a moment to feel into your meaningful story.
Breathe evenly and focus on your heart:

Things I feel truly grateful for:

Because...

What positive story will I tell:

I can express my gratitude by:

I can choose to focus on:

The difference I will make:

3 key emotions for me today:

*Give yourself a breath of thanks to remind yourself of the
gift of being alive. Then take a breath for each of the
people you care for.*

Pause. Take a moment to feel into your meaningful story.
Breathe evenly and focus on your heart:

Things I feel truly grateful for:

Because...

What positive story will I tell:

I can express my gratitude by:

I can choose to focus on:

The difference I will make:

3 key emotions for me today:

*Slowly turn the page in this journal and really listen
to the sound. What are you grateful for?*

Date: **Today's Context:**

Pause. Take a moment to feel into your meaningful story.
Breathe evenly and focus on your heart:

Things I feel truly grateful for:

Because...

What positive story will I tell:

I can express my gratitude by:

I can choose to focus on:

The difference I will make:

3 key emotions for me today:

"Piglet noticed that even though he had a very small heart,
it could hold a rather large amount of Gratitude"
- A.A. Milne

Date: **Today's Context:**

Pause. Take a moment to feel into your meaningful story.
Breathe evenly and focus on your heart:

Things I feel truly grateful for:

Because...

What positive story will I tell:

I can express my gratitude by:

I can choose to focus on:

The difference I will make:

3 key emotions for me today:

Pause. Take a moment to feel into your meaningful story.
Breathe evenly and focus on your heart:

Things I feel truly grateful for:

Because...

What positive story will I tell:

I can express my gratitude by:

I can choose to focus on:

The difference I will make:

3 key emotions for me today:

*"In ordinary life, we hardly realise that we receive a
great deal more than we give, and that it is only
with gratitude that life becomes rich"
- Dietrich Bonhoeffer*

Bonus Activity

The simple act of giving helps us feel more connected to others, which imbues our lives with a sense of meaning. By helping others and sharing our love, kindness, and compassion, we connect with the truth of who we are. And discover that even though on the surface we might all look very different from one another, at the core level we are all the same. Spend some time exploring the benefits of giving/serving e.g. feel calmer and happier, promote a sense of purpose, reduce pain etc. Which benefits resonate most with you?

There are many ways to help out a fellow human being today. These don't need to be grand gestures; even small, everyday behaviours can have a significant impact on others and on your own sense of well-being. The most important part of contributing to others, is the intention behind it which should always be to create happiness (or other positive intention) for the receiver – to give unconditionally and from the heart, without expectation. What ways can your contribute this week? For example, every time you meet someone, give them a joyful gift (a smile/compliment/silent blessing), express your love (via a hug/kind word), be present and listen, stop to help/give assistance etc.

"The heart that gives thanks is a happy one, for we cannot feel thankful and unhappy at the same time"
- Douglas Wood

35 Days in Review

Well done for completing 35 days. Take a moment to reflect on your achievements and to acknowledge your investment in YOU. Look back over your Journal entries from this week.

What are your key learnings, insights and discoveries from this week?

What changes in yourself have you been aware of? E.g. behaviours, focus, emotional state/mood etc.

What will you do differently next week?

Gratitude is a choice we make, an attitude we adopt.
You can choose to be grateful,
or ungrateful and take your gifts for granted.

GRATITUDE IS A powerful catalyst FOR Happiness. IT'S THE spark THAT lights A FIRE OF JOY in your soul.
AMY COLETTE

Date:　　　　　　**Today's Context:**

Pause. Take a moment to feel into your meaningful story.
Breathe evenly and focus on your heart:

Things I feel truly grateful for:

Because...

What positive story will I tell:

I can express my gratitude by:

I can choose to focus on:

The difference I will make:

3 key emotions for me today:

"Wear gratitude like a cloak,
and it will feed every corner of your life"
~ Rumi

Date: **Today's Context:**

Pause. Take a moment to feel into your meaningful story.
Breathe evenly and focus on your heart:

Things I feel truly grateful for:

Because...

What positive story will I tell:

I can express my gratitude by:

I can choose to focus on:

The difference I will make:

3 key emotions for me today:

Notice what you are touching right this moment.
What are you grateful for?

Date: **Today's Context:**

Pause. Take a moment to feel into your meaningful story.
Breathe evenly and focus on your heart:

Things I feel truly grateful for:

Because...

What positive story will I tell:

I can express my gratitude by:

I can choose to focus on:

The difference I will make:

3 key emotions for me today:

"Let us be grateful to the people who make us happy;
they are the charming gardeners who make our souls blossom"
~ Marcel Proust

Date: **Today's Context:**

Pause. Take a moment to feel into your meaningful story.
Breathe evenly and focus on your heart:

Day 39

Things I feel truly grateful for:

Because...

What positive story will I tell:

I can express my gratitude by:

I can choose to focus on:

The difference I will make:

3 key emotions for me today:

Date: **Today's Context:**

Pause. Take a moment to feel into your meaningful story.
Breathe evenly and focus on your heart:

Things I feel truly grateful for:

Because...

What positive story will I tell:

I can express my gratitude by:

I can choose to focus on:

The difference I will make:

3 key emotions for me today:

*Reach out and touch something smooth and then something
with real texture. What are you grateful for?*

Pause. Take a moment to feel into your meaningful story.
Breathe evenly and focus on your heart:

Things I feel truly grateful for:

Because...

What positive story will I tell:

I can express my gratitude by:

I can choose to focus on:

The difference I will make:

3 key emotions for me today:

*"True forgiveness is when you can say
'Thank you for the experience'"
~ Oprah Winfrey*

Date: **Today's Context:**

Pause. Take a moment to feel into your meaningful story.
Breathe evenly and focus on your heart:

Things I feel truly grateful for:

Because...

What positive story will I tell:

I can express my gratitude by:

I can choose to focus on:

The difference I will make:

3 key emotions for me today:

Alex de Tocqueville describes gratitude as "a habit of the heart".
How can you cultivate your heart habit even more deeply?

Bonus Activity

Daily Affirmations

Positive affirmations are declarations/short positive statements designed to be repeated to help you change the way you think, feel and behave. Although it might feel a little awkward saying them out loud for the first time, they are a great tool to rewire the brain to be more cheerful and optimistic (activating the same reward centres – ventral striatum and ventromedial prefrontal cortex – as other pleasurable experiences such as eating chocolate or winning a prize).

How to create affirmations:
Start with the words "I..." Use the present tense (even if it is something you wish to accomplish in the future) e.g. "I create..." Use a motivating adjective or verb to strengthen it. Be positive (affirming what you want, not what you don't want). Keep it short and specific. Make it realistic, achievable and meaningful.

We invite you to drop into your body and create affirmation(s) around something you want more of in life – something you can thoroughly get behind with your body/mind/soul. You might like to link them to your core values. Some examples are below:

I am treating myself with genuine respect and compassion each day.
I am more than enough, just the way I am.
I am opening my heart and drinking in the fully glory of this day.
I am using conscious balanced breathing as my anchor.
I am courageous and show up and let myself be seen.

To get the most out of affirmations, begin with balanced breathing. When you feel calm and alert, focus on saying them for 3-5 minutes using gut, heart and head awareness. Repeat each one approx 10 times, slowly, loudly and proudly (like you mean it, believe it, and as if it has already happened). Stay positive throughout the process. If you can, in your mind's eye, create a positive visualisation/mental rehearsal of the desired outcome, feelings, images, sounds etc.

How are you choosing to live in gratitude in this hour,
this day, this week, this month, this year of your life?

42 Days in Review

Well done for completing 42 days. Take a moment to reflect on your achievements and to acknowledge your investment in YOU. Look back over your Journal entries from this week.

What are your key learnings, insights and discoveries from this week?

What changes in yourself have you been aware of? E.g. behaviours, focus, emotional state/mood etc.

What will you do differently next week?

Bonus Activity

When we experience a set-back, it is common to become defensive and blame others or beat ourselves up with self-critical thoughts. Unfortunately, research shows neither response is helpful. Self-criticism is strongly related to depression and dissatisfaction with life. What if instead of judging ourselves, we treated ourselves with the same compassion and kindness we would a friend in a similar situation?

Dr Paul Gilbert (2014) defines compassion as *"a sensitivity to the suffering of self and others, with a commitment to try and relieve or prevent it"*. Dr Kristin Neff suggests that compassion is made up of three elements: self-kindness (vs. self-judgement); a sense of common humanity (vs. self as isolated); and mindfulness. Compassion isn't something soft, fluffy, weak or indulgent – it takes incredible courage and wisdom to be more kind to ourselves. And it has many positive benefits including: reduced shame, self-criticism and symptoms of anxiety/depression; improvements in self-worth and self-esteem; and increases in motivation to recover from failure.

Gilbert believes compassion flows in three directions: the compassion we offer to others (flowing out); the compassion we receive from others (flowing in); and the compassion we offer to ourselves (self-compassion). Yet most of us have never learned how to be gentle, kind and understanding with ourselves. Once you learn how to treat yourself as you treat your friends, life quickly becomes more joyful and meaningful. Like gratitude, it helps reduce the dominance of the threat system of the brain/body and increases the soothing systems capacity.

The use of compassionate imagery can be a powerful way to increase your ability to be self-compassionate. The following exercise is based on Paul Gilbert's *"Developing your compassionate self"* exercise. It involves visualising the part of you that is wise, strong and caring.

"If your compassion does not include yourself, it is incomplete"
- Buddha

Begin by finding a comfortable position, with a grounded, confident and open posture. Gently connect with a friendly facial expression. Bring your breathing into balance. When you are ready, like an actor getting into a role, use your imagination to create an image of who you would like to be as a compassionate person. It doesn't matter if you feel you are/aren't compassionate - the goal of this exercise is to imagine that you already have these qualities. When you feel ready, just allow an image to arise that represents compassion for you. Think/feel/identify the qualities/attributes/sensations/sounds you would have if you were compassionate.

You might like to imagine that your compassionate self is: wise; recognises that failure is a shared human experience; is kind when you fail and make mistakes; is strong, grounded and confident; shows care and concern for you; is committed to be helpful and supportive; is motivated to alleviate your own and others' suffering; accepts you for who you are; and demonstrates a sense of understanding for you and your feelings.

How might this version of you be/stand/hold its posture or move around? What might your facial expression be like as you embody your compassionate self? How would you like to sound? What would be a compassionate voice tone? Are there any other sensory qualities - colours and sounds? How might you interact and treat others?

Imagine now stepping into the shoes/body/mind of this truly compassionate version of you. How might you stand/move around as this wise, strong, caring, confident version of you? How would you treat other people given your kindness, care and desire to be helpful? And lastly, feel/think/identify how you might choose to treat yourself or someone else in a helpful, kind, caring way today.

When you have finished this exercise, write notes about what came up for you. Use these notes to begin to build your image further when you next repeat this exercise. Please note that creating your compassionate image may take a few attempts. So, take your time and go at your own pace.   For more exercises to help you develop your compassionate self, check out the resources section.

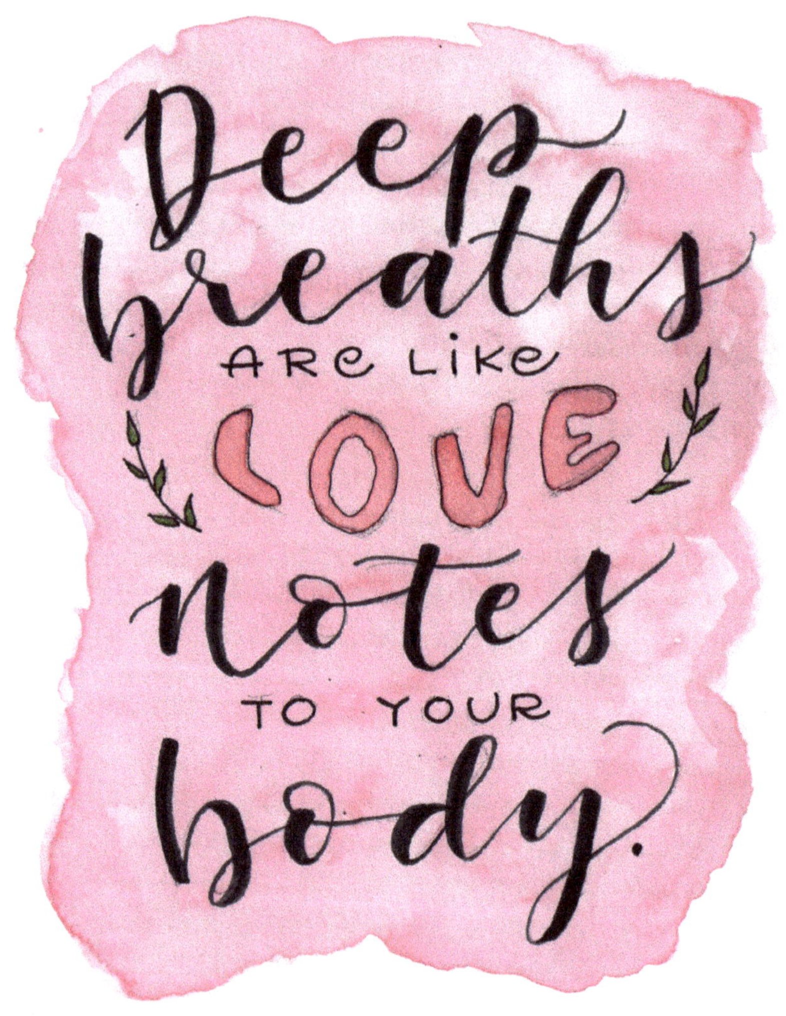
Deep breaths ARE LIKE LOVE notes TO YOUR body.

Pause. Take a moment to feel into your meaningful story.
Breathe evenly and focus on your heart:

Things I feel truly grateful for:

Because...

What positive story will I tell:

I can express my gratitude by:

I can choose to focus on:

The difference I will make:

3 key emotions for me today:

Pick up an object from your living room and feel the weight
of it in your hands. What are you grateful for?

Date: **Today's Context:**

Pause. Take a moment to feel into your meaningful story.
Breathe evenly and focus on your heart:

Things I feel truly grateful for:

Because...

What positive story will I tell:

I can express my gratitude by:

I can choose to focus on:

The difference I will make:

3 key emotions for me today:

*"Cultivate the habit of being grateful for every good thing
that comes to you, and to give thanks continuously.
And because all things have contributed to your advancement,
you should include all things in your gratitude"
~ Ralph Waldo Emerson*

Pause. Take a moment to feel into your meaningful story.
Breathe evenly and focus on your heart:

Things I feel truly grateful for:

Because...

What positive story will I tell:

I can express my gratitude by:

I can choose to focus on:

The difference I will make:

3 key emotions for me today:

*Can you recognise the gift of today as a new start,
a new day, a divine gift?*

Date: **Today's Context:**

Pause. Take a moment to feel into your meaningful story.
Breathe evenly and focus on your heart:

Things I feel truly grateful for:

Because...

What positive story will I tell:

I can express my gratitude by:

I can choose to focus on:

The difference I will make:

3 key emotions for me today:

In order to make room for more gratitude in your life,
what might you choose to let go of?

Date: **Today's Context:**

Pause. Take a moment to feel into your meaningful story.
Breathe evenly and focus on your heart:

Things I feel truly grateful for:

Because...

What positive story will I tell:

I can express my gratitude by:

I can choose to focus on:

The difference I will make:

3 key emotions for me today:

*"Let gratitude be the pillow upon which you kneel to say
your nightly prayer. And let faith be the bridge you
build to overcome evil and welcome good"*
- Maya Angelou

Pause. Take a moment to feel into your meaningful story.
Breathe evenly and focus on your heart:

Things I feel truly grateful for:

Because...

What positive story will I tell:

I can express my gratitude by:

I can choose to focus on:

The difference I will make:

3 key emotions for me today:

*"Gratitude is like a flashlight. If you go out in your yard at night and turn on a flashlight, you suddenly can see what's there.
It was always there but you couldn't see it in the dark"*
- Dawna Markova

Pause. Take a moment to feel into your meaningful story.
Breathe evenly and focus on your heart:

Things I feel truly grateful for:

Because...

What positive story will I tell:

I can express my gratitude by:

I can choose to focus on:

The difference I will make:

3 key emotions for me today:

Write down your favourite quote here.
What is it saying to you in your life, right now?

Bonus Activity

A "mantra" (affirming/positive phrase) in combination with breathing can be a great tool to support efforts towards experiencing a deeper state of inner quiet and peace. It helps to collect scattered attention, replacing 10,000 thoughts with just one. One of our favourites is *"Let it Be, Let it Go"* which was created by Mark Waldman.

Begin by checking in with your body and mind. Notice how you feel right now? Notice what your mind is doing.

Sit, stand or lie down. Begin to breathe deeply and slowly from the abdomen. Find the steady, balanced breathing rhythm that is now familiar to you. Allow the evenness of your breath to still your mind and act as a beacon to focus on when your mind begins to wander. As you inhale, say to yourself *"Let it Be"*. As you exhale, say to yourself "Let it Go". Continue to repeat this mantra in rhythm with your breath. As you inhale you might like to imagine your breath passing deep into your lungs and diaphragm; the words passing through the cells of your lung lining, and spreading through the whole body with each oxygen molecule. As you breathe out imagine anything that is not helpful, resourceful, healthy or of value, passing out of any part of the body / lungs with the carbon dioxide. Keep meditating in this way for 5-7 minutes and then rest quietly. Then take a moment to assess how you feel at head, heart and gut level.

49 Days in Review

Well done for completing 49 days. Take a moment to reflect on your achievements and to acknowledge your investment in YOU. Look back over your Journal entries from this week.

What are your key learnings, insights and discoveries from this week?

What changes in yourself have you been aware of? E.g. behaviours, focus, emotional state/mood etc.

What will you do differently next week?

"In the past I always thought of gratitude as a spontaneous response to the awareness of gifts received, but now I realise that gratitude can also be lived as a discipline. The discipline of gratitude is the explicit effort to acknowledge that all I am and have is given to me as a gift of love, a gift to be celebrated with joy"
- Henry Nouwen

Date: **Today's Context:**

Pause. Take a moment to feel into your meaningful story.
Breathe evenly and focus on your heart:

Things I feel truly grateful for:

Because...

What positive story will I tell:

I can express my gratitude by:

I can choose to focus on:

The difference I will make:

3 key emotions for me today:

The Latin root of the word gratitude is grata or gratia
– a gift freely given that is unearned.

Date: **Today's Context:**

Pause. Take a moment to feel into your meaningful story.
Breathe evenly and focus on your heart:

Things I feel truly grateful for:

Because...

What positive story will I tell:

I can express my gratitude by:

I can choose to focus on:

The difference I will make:

3 key emotions for me today:

"To be grateful is to recognise the love of God in everything"
~ Thomas Merton

Date: **Today's Context:**

Pause. Take a moment to feel into your meaningful story.
Breathe evenly and focus on your heart:

Things I feel truly grateful for:

Because...

What positive story will I tell:

I can express my gratitude by:

I can choose to focus on:

The difference I will make:

3 key emotions for me today:

The average person's skin covers an area of two metres^2
and accounts for approximately 15% of your body weight.
What are you grateful for?

Date: **Today's Context:**

Pause. Take a moment to feel into your meaningful story.
Breathe evenly and focus on your heart:

Things I feel truly grateful for: What positive story will I tell:

Because...

I can express my gratitude by: I can choose to focus on:

The difference I will make: 3 key emotions for me today:

*We must find time to stop and thank the people
who make a difference in our lives"
~ John F. Kennedy*

Pause. Take a moment to feel into your meaningful story.
Breathe evenly and focus on your heart:

Things I feel truly grateful for:

Because...

What positive story will I tell:

I can express my gratitude by:

I can choose to focus on:

The difference I will make:

3 key emotions for me today:

*"It is not happiness that makes us grateful,
but gratefulness that makes us happy"
~ Gratefulness.org*

Date: **Today's Context:**

Pause. Take a moment to feel into your meaningful story.
Breathe evenly and focus on your heart:

Things I feel truly grateful for:

Because...

I can express my gratitude by:

The difference I will make:

What positive story will I tell:

I can choose to focus on:

3 key emotions for me today:

"Gratitude is an experience of connection.
It is an emotion that exists in relationship with others and
that pulls us to want to deepen those relationships"
~ Deb Dana

Date: **Today's Context:**

Pause. Take a moment to feel into your meaningful story.
Breathe evenly and focus on your heart:

Things I feel truly grateful for:

Because...

What positive story will I tell:

I can express my gratitude by:

I can choose to focus on:

The difference I will make:

3 key emotions for me today:

"Gratitude is not only the greatest of virtues,
but the parent of all others"
~ Marcus Tullius Cicero

Align yourself
with people that
you can learn
from, people who
want more out of
life, people who
are stretching and
searching, and
seeking some
higher ground
in life.

LES BROWN

Bonus Activity

Self-care is about creating and maintaining practices that help you sustain your energy, spirit and being. It's about being a friend to yourself; and actively planning to include things in your day/week that re-fuel you. If you don't actively care for yourself, you won't be in a position to give to your loved ones either. Take some time to consider ways that you can take even better care of yourself? How do you currently take care of yourself and what might you want to include going forwards? Consider what activities nourish/energise/ground you. Which people help you feel loved, safe and ready to connect? What supportive places can you go to (either in reality or in your mind)? What practices do your friends do that you might like to try? Brainstorm these ideas and then write specific actions in the relevant column below. Some example activities:

- Physical: walking, gym, weights, swimming etc.
- Mental: learning something new, reading, debates, TED talks etc.
- Emotional: smile, gratitude, name your emotions, hug someone
- Social: coffee date, walk with a friend, dinner party
- Spiritual: prayer, meditation, be of service, connect

Date	Physical	Mental	Emotional	Social	Spiritual
Sunday					
Monday					
Tuesday					
Wedsday					
Thursday					
Friday					
Saturday					

You can download this planner at bit.ly/3PRn7L9

Your amazing heart will beat about 115,000 times each day without you having to think about it. What are you grateful for?

56 Days in Review

Well done for completing 56 days. Take a moment to reflect on your achievements and to acknowledge your investment in YOU. Look back over your Journal entries from this week.

What are your key learnings, insights and discoveries from this week?

What changes in yourself have you been aware of? E.g. behaviours, focus, emotional state/mood etc.

What will you do differently next week?

There are more than 500 million neurons in your gut –
it has its own nervous system. What are you grateful for?

Halfway Meaningful Story

You are now over halfway through this gratitude journal. Take a moment to stop and congratulate yourself for getting this far.

We imagine that you now have a more established practice in place and a narrative story that works well for you. You might like to consider experimenting by adding in another story or not – your choice. Here is one we love:

Story 4: The blind boy
A blind boy sat on the steps of a building with a hat and a sign by his feet which read, *"I am blind, please help."* There were just a few coins in the hat thrown in by folks as they hurried past. A woman walking by dropped some spare change into the hat. She then took the sign, and on the back wrote some words and put the sign back in the boy's hand so everyone could see the new words.

Soon the hat filled up with money and many more people gave generously. Later that day the woman returned to see how things were going. The boy recognised her footsteps and asked, *"Were you the one who changed my sign this morning?...What did you write?"*

The woman said, *"I said what you said but in a different way. I wrote, 'Today is a beautiful day, but I cannot see it.'"* Both signs spoke the truth. But the first sign simply said the boy was blind, while the second sign spoke to the hearts of everyone walking by, firing up feelings of how grateful they are to be able to see the beauty of the day...

Jot down: What are the main points of note in this story? What was the struggle? How did the woman help? How did it make you feel? Imagine you were the woman/the blind boy, how would you feel? What is the emotional impact of this story on you?

Pause. Take a moment to feel into your meaningful story. Breathe evenly and focus on your heart:

Things I feel truly grateful for:

Because...

What positive story will I tell:

I can express my gratitude by:

I can choose to focus on:

The difference I will make:

3 key emotions for me today:

"Gratitude looks to the past and love to the present;
fear, avarice, lust, and ambition look ahead"
~ C.S. Lewis

Pause. Take a moment to feel into your meaningful story. Breathe evenly and focus on your heart:

Things I feel truly grateful for:

Because...

What positive story will I tell:

I can express my gratitude by:

I can choose to focus on:

The difference I will make:

3 key emotions for me today:

When it's dark, walk outside and stand there for one minute looking up at the 200-400 billion stars in our galaxy. Contemplate how amazing life is.

Date: **Today's Context:**

Pause. Take a moment to feel into your meaningful
story. Breathe evenly and focus on your heart:

Things I feel truly grateful for:

Because...

What positive story will I tell:

I can express my gratitude by:

I can choose to focus on:

The difference I will make:

3 key emotions for me today:

*"The unthankful heart discovers no mercies; but the thankful
heart will find, in every hour, some heavenly blessings"
~ Henry Ward Beecher*

Date: **Today's Context:**

Pause. Take a moment to feel into your meaningful story. Breathe evenly and focus on your heart:

Things I feel truly grateful for:

Because...

What positive story will I tell:

I can express my gratitude by:

I can choose to focus on:

The difference I will make:

3 key emotions for me today:

Reflect on how it feels to have a roof over your head and a warm home. What are you grateful for?

Date: **Today's Context:**

Pause. Take a moment to feel into your meaningful story. Breathe evenly and focus on your heart:

Day 61

Things I feel truly grateful for:

Because...

What positive story will I tell:

I can express my gratitude by:

I can choose to focus on:

The difference I will make:

3 key emotions for me today:

What are the small pleasures you enjoy – a sunrise, a walk in the woods, a dip in the ocean, the sun warming your face?

Date: **Today's Context:**

Pause. Take a moment to feel into your meaningful story. Breathe evenly and focus on your heart:

Things I feel truly grateful for:

Because...

What positive story will I tell:

I can express my gratitude by:

I can choose to focus on:

The difference I will make:

3 key emotions for me today:

"When it comes to life, the critical thing is whether you take things for granted or take them with gratitude"
~ G.K. Chesterton

Date: **Today's Context:**

Pause. Take a moment to feel into your meaningful
story. Breathe evenly and focus on your heart:

Day 63

Things I feel truly grateful for:

Because...

What positive story will I tell:

I can express my gratitude by:

I can choose to focus on:

The difference I will make:

3 key emotions for me today:

*Focus on the gifts given by your friends and family – love,
support, kindness, fun...and then focus on what you give them.*

63 Days in Review

Well done for completing 63 days. Take a moment to reflect on your achievements and to acknowledge your investment in YOU. Look back over your Journal entries from this week.

What are your key learnings, insights and discoveries from this week?

What changes in yourself have you been aware of? E.g. behaviours, focus, emotional state/mood etc.

What will you do differently next week?

Bonus Activity

5-4-3-2-1 Senses Grounding Practice

Jon Kabat-Zinn defines mindfulness as *"paying attention in a particular way: on purpose, in the present moment, and non-judgmentally"*. It is not a way of making your mind quiet, but a way of entering into the quiet that is already there (buried under the 6,200+ thoughts the average person thinks every day). Mindfulness is evidence-based with thousands of studies documenting the physical and mental health benefits such as improving sleep, attention, productivity, focus, mood, empathy etc.

Mindfulness is a quality you already have, you just have to learn how to cultivate it. There are many ways to practice it. The following technique uses your five senses to anchor you and ground you in the here and now. It is profoundly simple, yet powerful as it helps calm anxious thoughts, reorientates you to the present and enables you to feel safe and in control.

  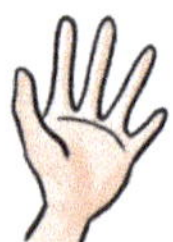  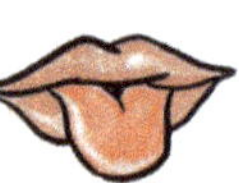

- Sit in a quiet space and set an intention to focus on you for five minutes (you can extend the time as you practice and become more comfortable and familiar with the process). Ideally, do this exercise barefooted.

- Place your feet flat on the floor. Really feel your connection to the ground. Focus on the sensation of the earth beneath your feet. Imagine the energy of your body flowing down into the solid, pure, reliable earth – like roots coming from a mighty tree trunk. Let your body feel and absorb the earth's qualities that you need most in this moment e.g. calm, reliability, safety...

- Become mindful of your breath inviting your body back into the moment, slowing everything down. Breathe deeply and evenly, as you know how to do now – six seconds in, six seconds out (or whatever count feels right for you), feeling a positive emotion in the area surrounding your heart.

- Moving only your eyes, look around and describe out loud five things you can see e.g. a tall solid tree with large branches swaying in the wind, the faded white paint on the windowsill etc. Describe the characteristics of each thing you see – colour, shape, size, consistency, location etc.

- Focusing on your body, describe four things you can feel e.g. the ring on your finger, the ground beneath you, a gentle breeze, the warmth of the sun on your skin etc. Pay attention to the way it might feel against your hand, its texture, temperature, weight, pressure etc.

- As you continue to evenly breathe, describe three things you can hear (if necessary closing your eyes as you do this to amplify your awareness) e.g. birds chirping, children playing, your breath etc. Notice the qualities of the sounds e.g. pitch, tone, cadence, tempo, volume, rhythm etc.

- Notice if there is anything you can smell. Describe two things you can smell (if you can't smell anything name your two favourite smells) e.g. the chocolatey leftover smell from dessert, a fresh vase of flowers, fresh-baked bread etc. Describe its attributes e.g. nutty, floral, spicy, citrus, burnt etc.

- Notice one thing you can taste e.g. minty toothpaste, the sharp orange juice from breakfast etc. If you can't taste anything, then name something you'd love to taste right now and describe its qualities e.g. sweet, bitter, salty, sour, astringent etc.

- End this exercise with one deep six second inhale and exhale.

You can repeat this as many times as you like, so that over time it becomes a familiar way to quickly and easily ground/settle yourself into the present moment.

Just Be
~ IN ~
a world full of
doing, doing, doing.
It's important to
take a moment
~ TO ~
just breathe,
to just be.

Date: **Today's Context:**

Pause. Take a moment to feel into your meaningful story.
Breathe evenly and focus on your heart:

Things I feel truly grateful for:

Because...

What positive story will I tell:

I can express my gratitude by:

I can choose to focus on:

The difference I will make:

3 key emotions for me today:

*How have the people and situations you have encountered
in your daily life awakened gratitude in your heart?*

Date: **Today's Context:**

Pause. Take a moment to feel into your meaningful story.
Breathe evenly and focus on your heart:

Things I feel truly grateful for: What positive story will I tell:

Because...

I can express my gratitude by: I can choose to focus on:

The difference I will make: 3 key emotions for me today:

*"The soul that gives thanks can find comfort in everything;
the soul that complains can find comfort in nothing"
~ Hannah Whitall Smith*

Date: **Today's Context:**

Pause. Take a moment to feel into your meaningful story.
Breathe evenly and focus on your heart:

Things I feel truly grateful for:

Because...

What positive story will I tell:

I can express my gratitude by:

I can choose to focus on:

The difference I will make:

3 key emotions for me today:

Date: **Today's Context:**

Pause. Take a moment to feel into your meaningful story.
Breathe evenly and focus on your heart:

Things I feel truly grateful for:

Because...

What positive story will I tell:

I can express my gratitude by:

I can choose to focus on:

The difference I will make:

3 key emotions for me today:

*"Gratitude is a powerful catalyst for happiness.
It's the spark that lights a fire of joy in your soul"
- Amy Collette*

Date: **Today's Context:**

Pause. Take a moment to feel into your meaningful story.
Breathe evenly and focus on your heart:

Things I feel truly grateful for:

Because...

What positive story will I tell:

I can express my gratitude by:

I can choose to focus on:

The difference I will make:

3 key emotions for me today:

*"If you fail to carry around with you a heart of gratitude
for the love you've been so freely given, it is easy for you
not to love others as you should"*
~ Paul David Tripp

Date: **Today's Context:**

Pause. Take a moment to feel into your meaningful story.
Breathe evenly and focus on your heart:

Things I feel truly grateful for:

Because...

What positive story will I tell:

I can express my gratitude by:

I can choose to focus on:

The difference I will make:

3 key emotions for me today:

*Practising gratitude helps rewire your brain to
think more positively, and in turn improves your
mood, satisfaction and overall happiness.*

Date: **Today's Context:**

Pause. Take a moment to feel into your meaningful story.
Breathe evenly and focus on your heart:

Things I feel truly grateful for:

Because...

What positive story will I tell:

I can express my gratitude by:

I can choose to focus on:

The difference I will make:

3 key emotions for me today:

70 Days in Review

Well done for completing 70 days. Take a moment to reflect on your achievements and to acknowledge your investment in YOU. Look back over your Journal entries from this week.

What are your key learnings, insights and discoveries from this week?

What changes in yourself have you been aware of? e.g. behaviours, focus, emotional state / mood etc.

What will you do differently next week?

Bonus Activity

Understanding and recognising emotion is vital for our well-being. Emotions aren't good or bad as they are just energy in motion that comes and goes. They are a signal we need to pay attention to.

Write down the 10 emotions you use most frequently around the diagram. You might like to use some of the words here based on eight basic emotions (fear, anger, sadness, joy, disgust, surprise, trust, anticipation), from Plutchik's Wheel of Emotions.

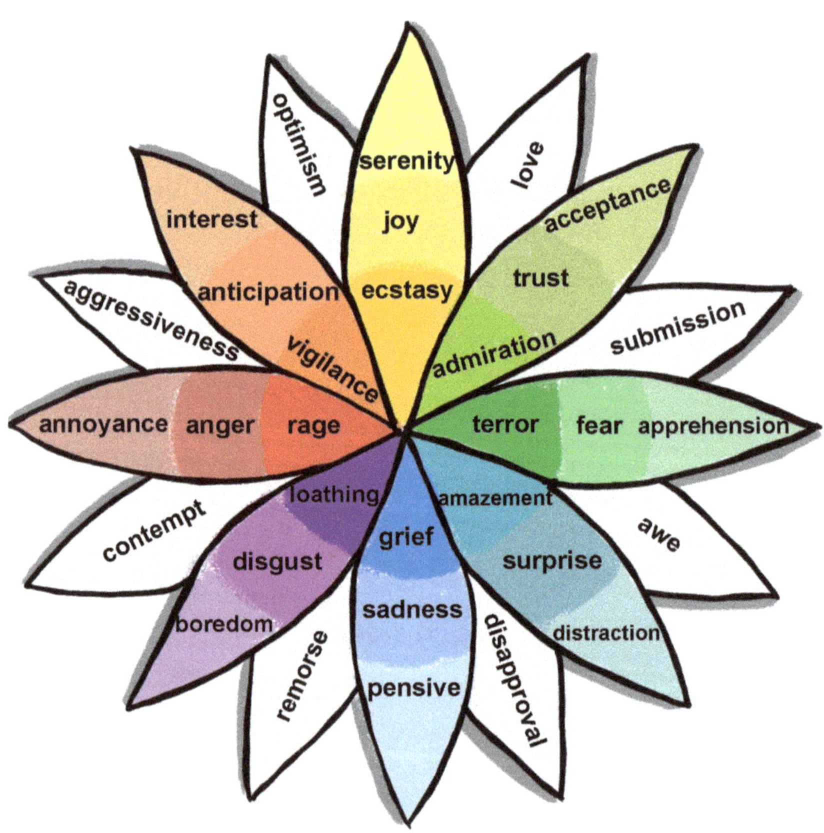

Think of emotions as your allies. They:
* ILLUMINATE what's important to you.
* MOTIVATE you to do something.
* COMMUNICATE to others what's going on for you.

Checking in with yourself and putting words to an emotion you are experiencing can change the experience and stop you from being caught up and swept away by an emotional tidal wave. It also creates a pause which helps you to find space to choose how you respond to challenges. For example, when your mind and body feels tense, do your best to attach words to the experience – *"I notice I am feeling agitated"*. You might then decide to release the emotion by imagining it leaving your body each time you exhale.

Try to go beyond the obvious first word you think of to identify exactly what you are feeling. For example:

- *Confusion:* Uncertain, upset, doubtful, indecisive, perplexed, embarrassed, hesitant, shy, lost, unsure, tense.
- *Anger:* Grumpy, frustrated, agitated, annoyed, defensive, spiteful, impatient, disgusted, offended, irritated, mad, livid.
- *Sad:* Disappointed, dejected, mournful, regretful, depressed, paralysed, pessimistic, tearful, dismayed, disillusioned, heavy, crushed.
- *Anxious:* Afraid, stressed, vulnerable, confused, bewildered, skeptical, worried, cautious, nervous.
- *Hurt:* Jealous, betrayed, let down, tender, wounded, impaired, damaged, criticised, abused, punished, rejected.
- *Happy:* thankful, trusting, comfortable, content, excited, relaxed, relieved, elated, confident.
- *Strong:* Certain, sure, dynamic, hardy, tenacious, empowered, ambitious, powerful, confident, bold, determined.
- *Energised:* Motivated, invigorated, focused, strengthened, determined, inspired, creative, renewed, vibrant, refreshed.

If you practice gratitude a little, your life will change a little. If you practice gratitude a lot everyday, your life will change dramatically and in ways that you can hardly imagine.

RHONDA BYRNE

Be Thankful

Be thankful that you don't already have everything you desire,
if you did, what would there be to look forward to?

Be thankful when you don't know something,
for it gives you the opportunity to learn.

Be thankful for the difficult times,
during those times you grow.

Be thankful for your limitations,
because they give you opportunities for improvement.

Be thankful for each new challenge,
because it will build your strength and character.

Be thankful for your mistakes,
they will teach you valuable lessons.

Be thankful when you're tired and weary,
because it means you've made a difference.

It is easy to be thankful for the good things.
A life of rich fulfilment comes to those who
are also thankful for the setbacks.

~ Unknown Author

Pause. Take a moment to feel into your meaningful story.
Breathe evenly and focus on your heart:

Things I feel truly grateful for:

Because...

What positive story will I tell:

I can express my gratitude by:

I can choose to focus on:

The difference I will make:

3 key emotions for me today:

"Gratitude and attitude are not challenges;
they are choices"
~ Robert Braathe

Date: **Today's Context:**

Pause. Take a moment to feel into your meaningful story.
Breathe evenly and focus on your heart:

Day 72

Things I feel truly grateful for:

Because...

What positive story will I tell:

I can express my gratitude by:

I can choose to focus on:

The difference I will make:

3 key emotions for me today:

*Your body is amazing. It helps you to walk, talk,
listen, see, hug, kiss, think, feel, breathe and
experience the world every single day.*

Date: **Today's Context:**

Pause. Take a moment to feel into your meaningful story.
Breathe evenly and focus on your heart:

Things I feel truly grateful for:

Because...

What positive story will I tell:

I can express my gratitude by:

I can choose to focus on:

The difference I will make:

3 key emotions for me today:

*"We can only be said to be alive in those moments
when our hearts are conscious of our treasures"
~ Thornton Wilder*

Date: **Today's Context:**

Pause. Take a moment to feel into your meaningful story.
Breathe evenly and focus on your heart:

Things I feel truly grateful for:

Because...

What positive story will I tell:

I can express my gratitude by:

I can choose to focus on:

The difference I will make:

3 key emotions for me today:

How are your frustrations, disappointments and challenges
mingling with your daily gratitude practice?

Date: **Today's Context:**

Pause. Take a moment to feel into your meaningful story.
Breathe evenly and focus on your heart:

Things I feel truly grateful for:

Because...

What positive story will I tell:

I can express my gratitude by:

I can choose to focus on:

The difference I will make:

3 key emotions for me today:

"Joy is the simplest form of gratitude"
~ Karl Barth

Date: **Today's Context:**

Pause. Take a moment to feel into your meaningful story.
Breathe evenly and focus on your heart:

Things I feel truly grateful for:

Because...

What positive story will I tell:

I can express my gratitude by:

I can choose to focus on:

The difference I will make:

3 key emotions for me today:

"Gratitude is the sign of noble souls"
~ Aesop

Date: **Today's Context:**

Pause. Take a moment to feel into your meaningful story.
Breathe evenly and focus on your heart:

Things I feel truly grateful for:

Because...

What positive story will I tell:

I can express my gratitude by:

I can choose to focus on:

The difference I will make:

3 key emotions for me today:

What ways has your perspective already shifted
from looking at what isn't working, to what is
working and all that is good in your life?

77 Days in Review

Well done for completing 77 days. Take a moment to reflect on your achievements and to acknowledge your investment in YOU. Look back over your Journal entries from this week.

What are your key learnings, insights and discoveries from this week?

What changes in yourself have you been aware of? E.g. behaviours, focus, emotional state/mood etc.

What will you do differently next week?

Bonus Activity

Gratitude Letter

Expressing gratitude brings positive emotions to both the people who give, and those who receive thanks. Yet we rarely fully express that gratitude to the people in our lives.

Choose someone in your life who has had a tremendous influence on you or who has been kind and helpful to you, but to whom you have never/rarely expressed your deep gratitude. They might be a partner/parent/child/grandparent/friend/mentor/colleague – anyone who has made a positive impact on your life. As you bring your breathing into balance, think, feel and identify specific things that this person has done that you are extremely grateful for.

Now find a pen and paper and write them a letter. Address the letter specifically to the person (e.g. Dear ...). Express your appreciation for what they have done and how they have impacted your life. Describe specific things that you are grateful for, how their behaviour has affected you, how they helped and what a difference they have made to your life. Don't worry about grammar and spelling, just let it flow from your heart. End the letter in a way that identifies it is from you (e.g. Sincerely..., or Love...,).

If you can, deliver the letter personally and read it to them or ask them to read the letter in your presence. You might like to use the space below to creates notes about what you will include:

gratitude
MAKES
sense OF OUR past,
BRINGS
peace FOR today,
AND CREATES A
vision FOR
tomorrow.
MELODIE BEATTIE

Date: **Today's Context:**

Pause. Take a moment to feel into your meaningful story.
Breathe evenly and focus on your heart:

Things I feel truly grateful for:

Because...

What positive story will I tell:

I can express my gratitude by:

I can choose to focus on:

The difference I will make:

3 key emotions for me today:

Run your fingertips along the skin and hairs on your arm.
Feel the gentle touch of your hand. What are you grateful for?

Date: **Today's Context:**

Pause. Take a moment to feel into your meaningful story.
Breathe evenly and focus on your heart:

Things I feel truly grateful for:

Because...

What positive story will I tell:

I can express my gratitude by:

I can choose to focus on:

The difference I will make:

3 key emotions for me today:

"Rest and be thankful"
~ William Wordsworth

Pause. Take a moment to feel into your meaningful story.
Breathe evenly and focus on your heart:

Things I feel truly grateful for:

Because...

What positive story will I tell:

I can express my gratitude by:

I can choose to focus on:

The difference I will make:

3 key emotions for me today:

*Gratitude invites us towards radical self-acceptance –
to fully embrace and accept ourselves wherever we are.*

Date: **Today's Context:**

Pause. Take a moment to feel into your meaningful story.
Breathe evenly and focus on your heart:

Things I feel truly grateful for:

Because...

What positive story will I tell:

I can express my gratitude by:

I can choose to focus on:

The difference I will make:

3 key emotions for me today:

*"I lie in bed at night, after ending my prayers with the words
"Thank you, God, for all that is good and dear and beautiful"
- Anne Frank*

Date: **Today's Context:**

Pause. Take a moment to feel into your meaningful story.
Breathe evenly and focus on your heart:

Things I feel truly grateful for:

Because...

I can express my gratitude by:

The difference I will make:

What positive story will I tell:

I can choose to focus on:

3 key emotions for me today:

"O Lord that lends me life, lend me
a heart replete with thankfulness"
- William Shakespeare

Date: **Today's Context:**

Pause. Take a moment to feel into your meaningful story.
Breathe evenly and focus on your heart:

Things I feel truly grateful for:

Because...

What positive story will I tell:

I can express my gratitude by:

I can choose to focus on:

The difference I will make:

3 key emotions for me today:

Give back to others in your community.
Volunteering not only helps others but increases our
feelings of social connection and wellbeing.

Date: **Today's Context:**

Pause. Take a moment to feel into your meaningful story.
Breathe evenly and focus on your heart:

Things I feel truly grateful for:

Because...

What positive story will I tell:

I can express my gratitude by:

I can choose to focus on:

The difference I will make:

3 key emotions for me today:

"Worry does not empty tomorrow of its sorrow,
it empties today of its strength"
- Corrie Ten Boom

Do not be
anxious about
anything, but
in every situation
by prayer and petition
with thanksgiving
present your requests
to God.

PHILIPPIANS 4:6

84 Days in Review

Well done for completing 84 days. Take a moment to reflect on your achievements and to acknowledge your investment in YOU. Look back over your Journal entries from this week.

What are your key learnings, insights and discoveries from this week?

What changes in yourself have you been aware of? E.g. behaviours, focus, emotional state/mood etc.

What will you do differently next week?

Gratitude is not about "fake it till you make it". Giving and receiving thanks must be genuine for you to receive the benefits.

Bonus Activity

The Jar of Awesome was an idea created by Tim Ferris to celebrate the small wins that happen every day (that you often forget about) and keep you motivated when things get tough.

Find a big, clean glass jar and write 'Jar of Awesome' on it. Whenever something great happens (a success no matter how small), write it on a slip of paper e.g. tightened your belt buckle another notch, meditated three days in a row etc. Fold the paper into a small square and put your 'small win' into the Jar of Awesome. You can do this on your own, with a partner/wider family/friends/work colleagues.

The idea is to keep collecting these positive nuggets so when you find yourself feeling down/needing motivation, all you have to do is pull out a random note and read it to realise you do have things to celebrate. And as you continue to grow and accomplish more, you'll be able to periodically look back through your positive memories and reflect on all that you've learned and accomplished.

Why don't you try it out for the next week. Start on Monday and spend a minute writing some of your small wins and achievements. Then in one month from now, take the notes out and revisit them. As you read them and connect with them in your heart, you might like to write key ones in your Journal.

Blow gently on your hands like you're blowing bubbles.
Feel your breath as it hits your hands. What are you grateful for?

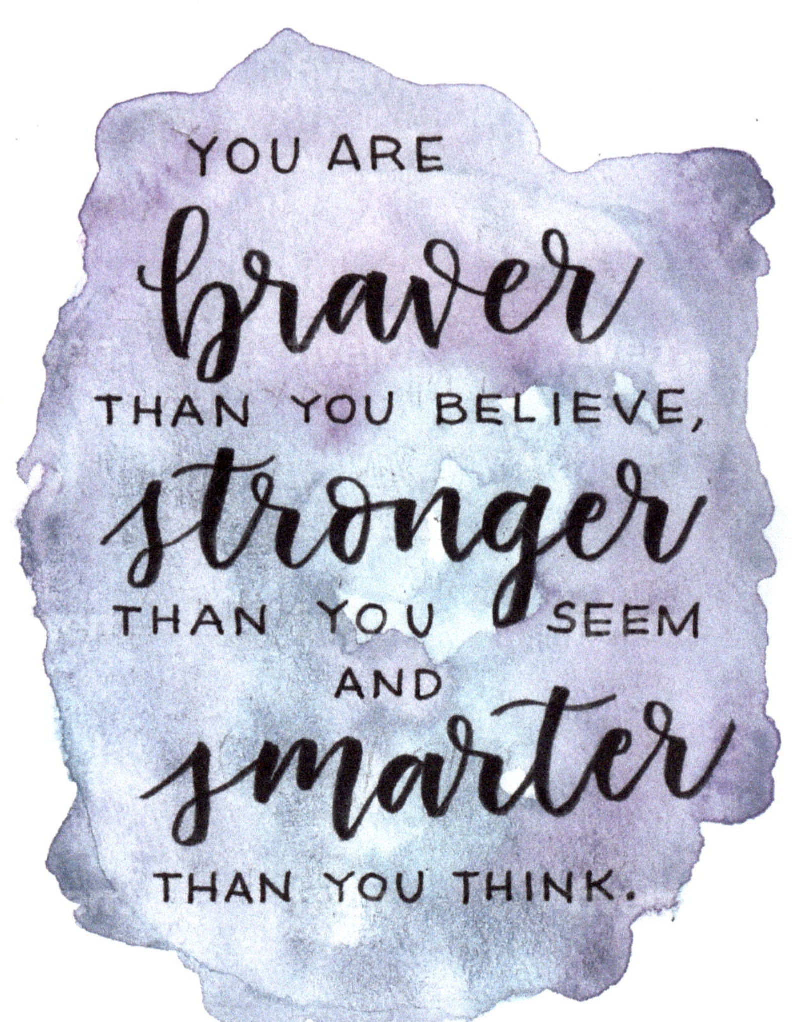
YOU ARE
braver
THAN YOU BELIEVE,
stronger
THAN YOU SEEM
AND
smarter
THAN YOU THINK.

Date: **Today's Context:**
Pause. Take a moment to feel into your meaningful story.
Breathe evenly and focus on your heart:

Things I feel truly grateful for:

Because...

What positive story will I tell:

I can express my gratitude by:

I can choose to focus on:

The difference I will make:

3 key emotions for me today:

"I'm still thanking all the stars, one by one"
- Marissa Meyer

Date: **Today's Context:**

Pause. Take a moment to feel into your meaningful story.
Breathe evenly and focus on your heart:

Things I feel truly grateful for:

Because...

What positive story will I tell:

I can express my gratitude by:

I can choose to focus on:

The difference I will make:

3 key emotions for me today:

How do you express your gratitude to others?

Date: **Today's Context:**

Pause. Take a moment to feel into your meaningful story.
Breathe evenly and focus on your heart:

Things I feel truly grateful for:

Because...

What positive story will I tell:

I can express my gratitude by:

I can choose to focus on:

The difference I will make:

3 key emotions for me today:

*"Gratitude bestows reverence...changing forever
how we experience life and the world"
~ John Milton*

Date: **Today's Context:**

Pause. Take a moment to feel into your meaningful story.
Breathe evenly and focus on your heart:

Things I feel truly grateful for:

Because...

What positive story will I tell:

I can express my gratitude by:

I can choose to focus on:

The difference I will make:

3 key emotions for me today:

"Gratitude goes beyond the 'mine' and 'thine'
and claims the truth that all of life is a pure gift"
~ Henri Nouwen

Date: **Today's Context:**

Pause. Take a moment to feel into your meaningful story.
Breathe evenly and focus on your heart:

Things I feel truly grateful for:

Because...

What positive story will I tell:

I can express my gratitude by:

I can choose to focus on:

The difference I will make:

3 key emotions for me today:

Write a list of all the people who have been a
blessing to you in the last year. Then make the
effort to call them up/write and tell them.

Date: **Today's Context:**

Pause. Take a moment to feel into your meaningful story.
Breathe evenly and focus on your heart:

Day 90

Things I feel truly grateful for:

Because...

What positive story will I tell:

I can express my gratitude by:

I can choose to focus on:

The difference I will make:

3 key emotions for me today:

"Appreciation can make a day, even change a life.
Your willingness to put it into words is all that is necessary"
~ Margaret Cousins

Date: **Today's Context:**

Pause. Take a moment to feel into your meaningful story.
Breathe evenly and focus on your heart:

Things I feel truly grateful for:

What positive story will I tell:

Because...

I can express my gratitude by:

I can choose to focus on:

The difference I will make:

3 key emotions for me today:

Gratitude reduces a multitude of toxic emotions,
from resentment to frustration, envy and regret.

91 Days in Review

Well done for completing 91 days. Take a moment to reflect on your achievements and to acknowledge your investment in YOU. Look back over your Journal entries from this week.

What are your key learnings, insights and discoveries from this week?

What changes in yourself have you been aware of? E.g. behaviours, focus, emotional state/mood etc.

What will you do differently next week?

"By taking just a few extra seconds to stay with
a positive experience — even the comfort in a single
breath — you'll help turn a passing mental
state into lasting neural structure"
~ Rick Hanson

Bonus Activity

When was the last time you had fun? When you indulged in an activity

that was purposeless, fun and pleasurable? Or when you lost yourself in something really engaging/absorbing?

Play is just as important for adults as it is for kids. It is a great source of joy, relaxation, and flow. It engages the creative parts of the brain and silences your inner critic – which can often sensor great new thoughts and ideas. And it is vital for problem solving and relationships.

How can you create opportunities to play more? To forget about work and commitments, be social, use your imagination, problem solve and engage in fun and laughter. This week, set a goal to be social, to play more. Surround yourself with playful people. Hang out with kids. Play with Lego. Unwind with mindful colouring. Go to the movies. Host a games night. Play with a pet. Joke with strangers. Learn a magic trick. Do something that makes you smile from the inside out. George Bernard Shaw once said, *"We don't stop playing because we grow old; we grow old because we stop playing"*.

Smiling is contagious. When someone is having
a rough day, give them your best smile
as not only will they feel better but so will you ☺

Start
each day
with a
grateful
heart.

Date: **Today's Context:**

Pause. Take a moment to feel into your meaningful story.
Breathe evenly and focus on your heart:

Things I feel truly grateful for:

Because...

What positive story will I tell:

I can express my gratitude by:

I can choose to focus on:

The difference I will make:

3 key emotions for me today:

*"Don't let the sun go down without saying thank you
to someone, and without admitting to yourself that
absolutely no one gets this far alone"*
- Stephen King

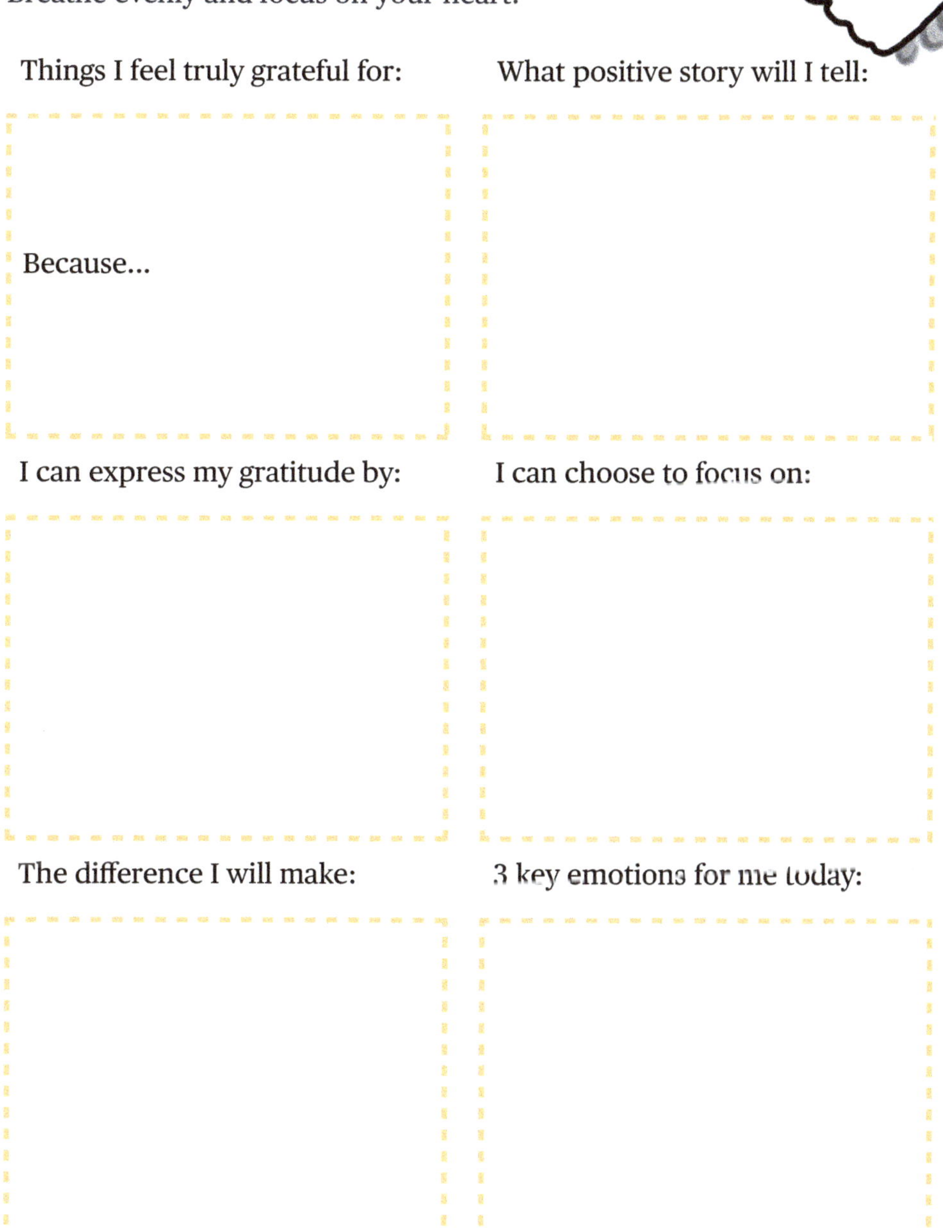

Date: **Today's Context:**

Pause. Take a moment to feel into your meaningful story.
Breathe evenly and focus on your heart:

Things I feel truly grateful for:

Because...

What positive story will I tell:

I can express my gratitude by:

I can choose to focus on:

The difference I will make:

3 key emotions for me today:

It is not happy people who are thankful.
It is thankful people who are happy.

Date:　　　　　　　**Today's Context:**

Pause. Take a moment to feel into your meaningful story.
Breathe evenly and focus on your heart:

Things I feel truly grateful for:

Because...

What positive story will I tell:

I can express my gratitude by:

I can choose to focus on:

The difference I will make:

3 key emotions for me today:

"Happiness cannot be travelled to, owned, earned, worn or consumed. Happiness is the spiritual experience of living every minute with love, grace, and gratitude"
- Denis Waitley

Pause. Take a moment to feel into your meaningful story.
Breathe evenly and focus on your heart:

Things I feel truly grateful for:

Because...

What positive story will I tell:

I can express my gratitude by:

I can choose to focus on:

The difference I will make:

3 key emotions for me today:

Grateful people sleep better.
What are you thankful for when it comes to your sleep habits?

Date: **Today's Context:**

Pause. Take a moment to feel into your meaningful story.
Breathe evenly and focus on your heart:

Things I feel truly grateful for:

Because...

What positive story will I tell:

I can express my gratitude by:

I can choose to focus on:

The difference I will make:

3 key emotions for me today:

*In what ways can you expand your circle of gratitude to include
other qualities like joy, appreciation, compassion, creativity,
courage, generosity to everyone and
everything that you come into contact with?*

Date: **Today's Context:**

Pause. Take a moment to feel into your meaningful story.
Breathe evenly and focus on your heart:

Things I feel truly grateful for:

Because...

What positive story will I tell:

I can express my gratitude by:

I can choose to focus on:

The difference I will make:

3 key emotions for me today:

"The greatest gift one can give is thanksgiving.
In giving gifts, we give what we can spare,
but in giving thanks we give ourselves"
~ David Steindl-Rast

Date: **Today's Context:**

Pause. Take a moment to feel into your meaningful story.
Breathe evenly and focus on your heart:

Things I feel truly grateful for:

Because...

What positive story will I tell:

I can express my gratitude by:

I can choose to focus on:

The difference I will make:

3 key emotions for me today:

*Take a deep breath through each nostril in turn. Notice the
scents and smells around you. What are you grateful for?*

It is not
happy
people who
are thankful.
It is
thankful
people who
are happy.

Bonus Activity

Feel the gratitude in your heart as you go through the letters of the alphabet, from A to Z, and write down the things/people/attributes you are grateful for that start with each letter e.g. A - Adaptability, Avocados and Answered prayers; B - Bravado, Beauty in all its forms and being able to Breathe; C - Creativity, Coffee from my favourite mug and Cheesecake (my favourite dessert). If you find this easy, challenge yourself to find three + things for each letter.

Date: **Today's Context:**

Pause. Take a moment to feel into your meaningful story.
Breathe evenly and focus on your heart:

Things I feel truly grateful for:

Because...

What positive story will I tell:

I can express my gratitude by:

I can choose to focus on:

The difference I will make:

3 key emotions for me today:

*"I would maintain that thanks are the highest form of thought;
and that gratitude is happiness doubled by wonder."*
- G.K. Chesterton

Date: **Today's Context:**

Pause. Take a moment to feel into your meaningful story.
Breathe evenly and focus on your heart:

Things I feel truly grateful for:

Because...

What positive story will I tell:

I can express my gratitude by:

I can choose to focus on:

The difference I will make:

3 key emotions for me today:

*"We tend to routinely rush forward toward
the next good thing continuously which prevents
the current good things from sinking in"*
- Dr Rick Hanson

100 Days in Review

Well done for completing 100 days. You did it! Take a moment to reflect on your achievements and to acknowledge your investment in YOU. Look back over your Journal entries from this week.

What are your key learnings, insights and discoveries from this week?

What changes in yourself have you been aware of? E.g. behaviours, focus, emotional state/mood etc.

What will you do differently next week?

Practising Random Acts of Kindness boosts serotonin and reduces anxiety. Examples include really listening to others, to leaving a review on Amazon for a good book, to preparing a meal for someone.

Bonus Activity

Appreciating Yourself

When was the last time you truly, deeply appreciated you?

Begin by doing your balanced breathing, focus on your heart and write down what you appreciate about yourself: your strengths, your favourite characteristics, abilities and values. Take some time, deeply acknowledging yourself with positivity and tenderness. Focus on what you know inside of you – even if others don't appreciate all the same things.

Around the heart below, draw/write everything that you are grateful for about yourself.

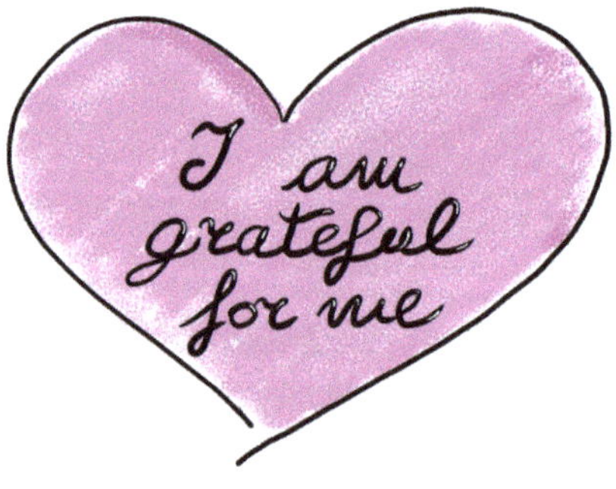

*"Gratitude is when memory is stored in
the heart and not in the mind"*

I AM *enough.*
YOU ARE *enough.*
I HAVE *always been enough.*
YOU HAVE *always been enough.*
INDEED I AM *more than enough.*
YOU ARE *more than enough.*
I AM *constantly changing, growing* AND *evolving.*
I HAVE *taken a lifetime learning* TO *love myself.*
I *pray* YOU WILL *get there much faster than me.*

SUZANNE HENWOOD

Reflecting Back

100 days ago you began a journey deep into gratitude. A potent gratitude practice that: stimulated your autonomic nervous system into a state of calm alertness; used storytelling (activating the pro-social circuit); and used your multiple brains to really savour and take in the good.

Whether you completed the whole 100 days/did less/took longer, it doesn't matter. This was always your journey to direct.

"A river cuts through rock not because of its power but because of its persistence" - James N. Watkins

We want to say, from our hearts to yours, *"bravo"*, *"well done"* and *"welcome"* to the new you – the more deeply connected you who has already rewired and brought about positive change...and no doubt will continue to do so.

Now is the time to take a deep breath, smile and celebrate the investment you have made in you. As L'Oréal said in their advertisements *"Because you're worth it"*. It is only right and fitting that you take time to acknowledge reaching this milestone.

Research shows that new habits take between 21 to 90 days to form. After 100 days you have intentionally created a new habit to deeply connect with yourself; challenged negative thinking patterns and reduced the defensive circuits; strengthened the wiring of the pro-social circuits in your brain (designed to bring you closer to yourself and others); and a whole host of other positive benefits.

Take a moment to reflect and write about what has changed for you. Notice what is new and different now – and what impact those differences have had on your life. What have others noticed?

It does not have to end here. We encourage you to begin your next 100 days. You cannot, as they say, step into the same river twice – the river will have changed and you will have changed. Begin a shiny new gratitude journal – and step in afresh. Talk to your friends/family/colleagues/those you care about and encourage them to join you. Just imagine where this could take you in another 100 days.

> *"We should certainly count our blessings,*
> *but we should also make our blessings count"*
> *- Neal A. Maxwell*

Reviewing the Journey

At the start of this journey, you took a moment to reflect on how life was for you. Without looking at what you wrote then – just breathe, focus on your heart and answer those same questions again. Mark for each statement, where you are on the scale: from 1 (strongly disagree), 2 (disagree), 3 (slightly disagree), 4 (neutral), 5 (slightly agree), 6 (agree) to 7 (strongly agree).*

	1	2	3	4	5	6	7
1. I have so much in life to be thankful for							
2. If I had to list everything that I felt grateful for, it would be a very long list							
3. When I look at the world, I don't see much to be grateful for							
4. I am grateful to a wide variety of							
5. As I get older I find myself more able to appreciate the people, events, and situations that have been part of my life							
6. Long amounts of time can go by before I feel grateful to something or someone							

Calculate your total score, by adding up each individual score of each question. Note that the scores from questions 3 and 6 are reverse-scored (i.e. count as a negative statement), so if the score in the first column is 7 then the score in the last column might be 1. Divide your total score by 6 to give you an average score. If you need more advice on scoring please visit www.theluminosityproject.nz

Record your new score here:

Now look back and see how things have changed. And do let us know, so we can celebrate with you.

Old score:

*Source: The Gratitude Questionnaire-Six-Item Form (GQ-6) by McCullough, M. E., Emmons, R. A., & Tsang, J.

At the start of this journey, you recorded three desired outcomes (on page 33). Get curious and ask yourself, did you achieve them? Or did they evolve? Did achieving them allow you to achieve what you wanted? You might like to draw yourself a certificate/congratulatory award to celebrate your progress.

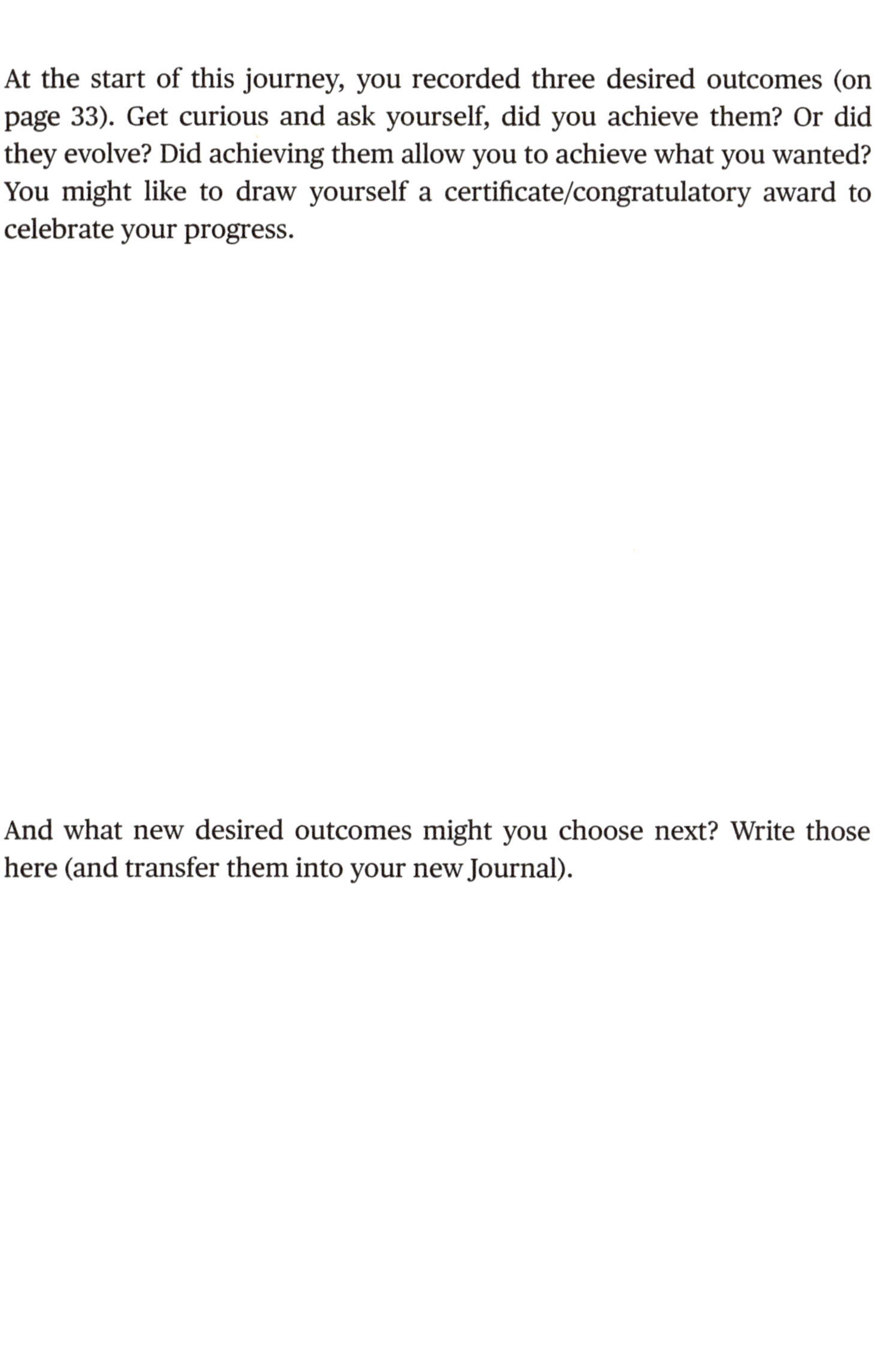

And what new desired outcomes might you choose next? Write those here (and transfer them into your new Journal).

"There is more to life than increasing its speed"
- Mahatma Gandhi

Links and Resources

Here are a few awesome resources to help you take this journey further.

Articles / Online Resources:

- Benefits of Gratitude, www.positivepsychology.com/benefits-of-gratitude/
- Compassion Based Therapy, Paul Gilbert https://www.compassionatemind.co.uk/resource/resources
- Conscious processing of narrative stimuli synchronises heart rate between individuals, 14 September 2021 https://www.sciencedirect.com/science/article/pii/S2211124721011396
- Giving thanks can make you happier, 14 August 2021 https://www.health.harvard.edu/healthbeat/giving-thanks-can-make-you-happier
- Grateful People Are Happy and Healthy – But Why? 28 Sept 2017 https://kids.frontiersin.org/articles/10.3389/frym.2017.00055
- Gratitude, Kelly McGonigal http://kellymcgonigal.com/gratitude
- Gratitude Survey to measure past appreciation www.authentichappiness.sas.upenn.edu/testcenter
- How Gratitude Changes You and Your Brain, 6 June 2017 https://greatergood.berkeley.edu/article/item/how_gratitude_changes_you_and_your_brain
- Manage Your Emotional Culture, Feb 2016 https://hbr.org/2016/01/manage-your-emotional-culture
- Neural Correlates of Gratitude, Glenn R Fox, Jonas Kaplan, Hanna Damasio, Antonio Damasio, 30 Sept 2015, https://pubmed.ncbi.nlm.nih.gov/26483740/
- Practicing gratitude can have profound health benefits, 25 Nov 2019 https://news.usc.edu/163123/gratitude-health-research-thanksgiving-usc-experts/
- Self-Compassion Guided Practices and Exercises, Kristin Neff https://self-compassion.org/category/exercises/#guided-meditations
- Science Proves That Gratitude Is Key to Well-Being: Acting happy coaxes one's brain toward positive emotions, 30 July 2018 https://www.psychologytoday.com/us/blog/mindful-anger/201807/science-proves-gratitude-is-key-well-being
- The Emotional Culture Deck https://www.ridersandelephants.com

- The Neuroscience of Gratitude and How It Affects Anxiety & Grief, 10 Sept 2021 https://positivepsychology.com/neuroscience-of-gratitude/
- The Science Of Gratitude: How Thankfulness Impacts Our Brains and Business, 22 Nov 2021 https://www.forbes.com/sites/kevinkruse/2021/11/22/the-science-of-gratitude-how-thankfulness-impacts-our-brains-and-business/?sh=5c5575152Occ
- The Science of Gratitude: New research suggests saying thanks regularly can benefit your health, 28 Nov 2013 https://nautil.us/issue/7/waste/the-science-of-gratitude
- What Parents Neglect to Teach about Gratitude, 21 Nov 2017 https://greatergood.berkeley.edu/article/item/what_parents_neglect_to_teach_about_gratitude
- Why Gratitude is Good by Robert Emmons, 16 November 2010 https://greatergood.berkeley.edu/article/item/why_gratitude_is_good

Books:

- Grateful: The Subversive Practice of Giving Thanks, Diana Butler Bass, 9 Apr 2019
- Hardwiring Happiness: The New Brain Science of Contentment, Calm, and Confidence, Rick Hanson PhD, 27 Dec 2016
- Neurodharma: New Science, Ancient Wisdom, and Seven Practices of the Highest Happiness, Rick Hanson PhD, 5 May 2020
- Thanks!: How Practicing Gratitude Can Make You Happier, Robert Emmons, 1 Nov 2008
- The Gratitude Project: How the Science of Thankfulness Can Rewire Our Brains for Resilience, Optimism, and the Greater Good, Jeremy Adam Smith , Kira M. Newman, et al., 1 Sep 2020

Listen to:

- An Experiment in Gratitude, The Science of Happiness (7 mins) https://www.youtube.com/watch?v=oHv6vTKD6lg
- Gratitude: The Short Film, Louie Schwartzberg (6 mins) https://www.youtube.com/watch?v=cpkEvBtyL7M
- The Power of Gratitude, Robert Emmons (8 mins) https://youtu.be/jLjVOvZufNM
- The Science of Gratitude (4 mins) https://www.youtube.com/watch?v=JMd1CcGZYwU

- The Science of Gratitude and How to Build a Gratitude Practice, Huberman Lab Podcast with Dr. Andrew Huberman, (1 hr 28 mins) https://hubermanlab.com/the-science-of-gratitude-and-how-to-build-a-gratitude-practice/

The Gratitude Questionnaire-Six-Item Form (GQ-6) https://ggsc.berkeley.edu/images/uploads/The_Gratitude_Questionnaire.pdf

Check out the book *"mBraining: using your multiple brains to do cool stuff"* by Grant Soosalu and Marvin Oka if you want to read more about the amazing field of mBraining.

www.theluminosityproject.nz
www.mBrainingtheworld.com
www.mbrainingglobal.com
www.the-healthy-workplace.com
www.mbraining4success.com
www.mbraining.com

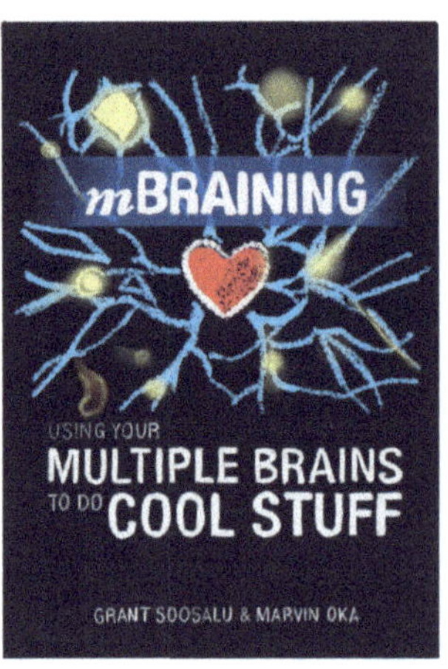

The above websites have a range of tips, tools, meditation downloads, talks, inspirational interviews, breathing pacers/guides and more. You can also find information on mBIT Coaching – an amazing suite of tools for enhancing what you do; coaching, self development, leadership, management, performance, teams, sports, stress, health, teaching, decision making etc. And information on how you can train as an mBIT Coach as well as contact details for Trainers and Coaches.

And again, well done for making it through this journey.

You are AMAZING!

Suzanne and Sarah x

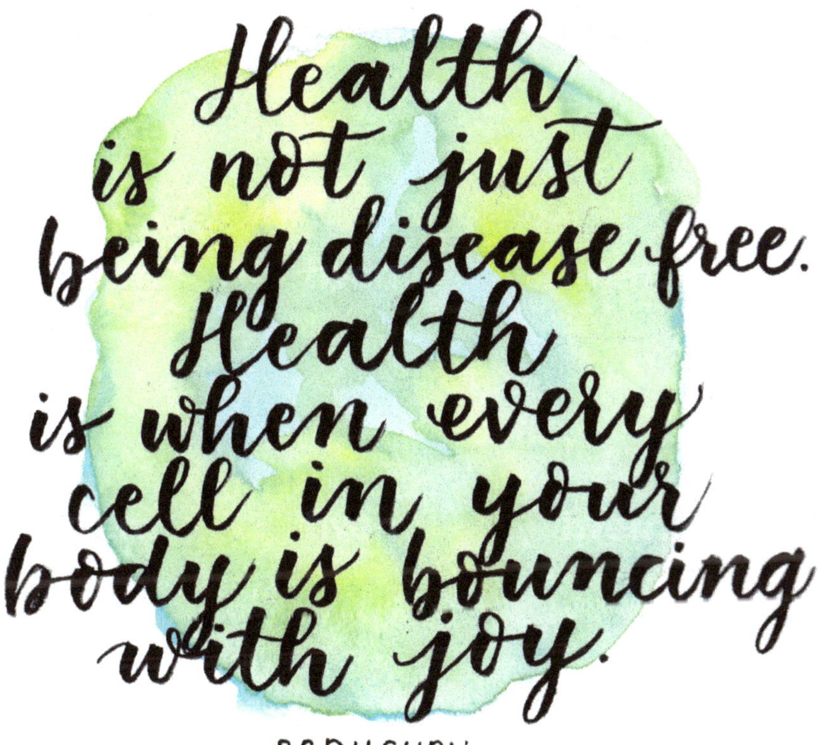

Health is not just being disease free.
Health is when every cell in your body is bouncing with joy.

SADHGURU

About Us

The Luminosity Project inspires, empowers and supports people to bring the best of who they are to everything they do – to let their light shine, creating a positive ripple effect in the world.   We help people on their journey to radical wholeness – to find the way back to themselves, each other and to source.

"Our deepest fear is not that we are inadequate.
Our deepest fear is that we are powerful beyond measure.
It is our light, not our darkness that most frightens us.
We ask ourselves, "Who am I to be brilliant,
gorgeous, talented, fabulous?"
Actually, who are you not to be?
You are a child of God.
Your playing small does not serve the world.
There is nothing enlightened about shrinking
so that other people won't feel insecure around you.
We are all meant to shine, as children do.
We were born to make manifest the glory of God that is within us.
It's not just in some of us; it's in everyone.
And as we let our own light shine,
we unconsciously give other people permission to do the same.
As we are liberated from our own fear,
our presence automatically liberates others"

- Marianne Williamson

Please feel free to get in touch if you would like to find out more
www.theluminosityproject.nz

Acknowledgements

This Gratitude Journal was concepted and co-created by Suzanne Henwood and Sarah Carruthers. However, it became a reality due to the time, energy, guidance, critique, inspiration and genius of many people.

So we take our hats off to...

Jana Branca
Ken Brinsdon
Rob Carruthers
Helen Davies
Karen Falconer
Grant Soosalu
Clive Teare
Phil Henwood
Sarah Thurley

Our Illustrator Eleonora D'Amico
https://www.instagram.com/eleofanta/

Our Calligraphy/Hand lettering artist Erlaine Gool
https://www.instagram.com/inkedbyerl/

And last but not least we would like to thank YOU, the person reading this Journal, for taking the steps to create a better YOU.

"Appreciation is a wonderful thing.
It makes what is excellent in others
belong to us as well"
~ Voltaire

In Loving Memory of

*For helping us to deeply
reconnect with ourselves.
We will forever be indebted to you.*

www.ingramcontent.com/pod-product-compliance
Lightning Source LLC
Chambersburg PA
CBHW052358030726

47599CB00014B/1120